CONTENTS

LB BOOKS

Published 2025. Little Brother Books Ltd, 23 Southernhay East, Exeter, Devon, EX1 1QL

books@littlebrotherbooks.co.uk | www.littlebrotherbooks.co.uk

Printed in Italy.
Little Brother Books, 77 Camden Street Lower, Dublin D02 XE80

The Little Brother Books trademarks, logos, email and website addresses and the GamesWarrior logo and imprint are sole and exclusive properties of Little Brother Books Limited.

QUIZ CORNER

We're dropping in with two puzzles to test your Battle Royale brainpower. Tackle our themed crossword, packed with clues from across the Island, then dive into the wordsearch to find hidden Fortnite favourites. Whether you're a casual looter or a full-on Victory Royale vet, there's something here for you. Ready up and get solving!

CROSSWORD

ANSWERS ON PAGE 77.

ACROSS

3 The Fortnite name for a custom outfit used to show off style (4)
4 A character with a golden touch who has been a big part of Fortnite storylines (5)
8 Slang for building rapidly during combat (5)
9 The ominous force surrounding the Island that gradually covers everything (5)
10 A close-range weapon that does lots of damage (7)
11 Fortnite's iconic banana skin with a goofy grin (5)

DOWN

1 What you use to make a safe descent from the Battle Bus at the start of each game (6)
2 A locked room on the Island that is filled with loot (5)
5 Fortnite's poster boy and one of the default skins (6)
6 _____ Towers, one of Fortnite's most iconic landing spots (6)
7 An inventory item you can lay to surprise opponents (4)
9 The blue juice that regenerates health and shield in Fortnite (5)
12 Victory dances and cheeky taunts are examples of what? (5)

WORDSEARCH

S	R	F	A	O	U	C	C	R	L	E	E	I	H
O	C	S	M	S	S	S	T	H	R	C	J	N	K	O
E	V	L	E	T	N	T	T	O	R	R	I	O	P
G	T	U	D	S	I	E	I	L	P	J	P	S	R
U	F	R	K	O	P	E	P	I	P	P	E	U	E
J	G	P	I	R	E	B	O	O	T	O	A	D	T
G	S	O	T	E	R	F	U	Y	P	R	R	S	I
U	N	L	O	R	E	R	U	E	T	V	G	N	N
H	O	R	O	Y	A	L	E	P	K	J	C	O	T
C	S	R	T	G	P	O	F	E	R	I	K	L	R
E	T	E	J	R	L	O	O	R	U	U	O	T	O
D	O	R	S	H	I	E	L	D	H	S	E	J	F
T	R	V	Y	E	E	Y	S	N	L	I	I	S	S
V	M	Y	Y	O	I	N	V	I	C	T	O	R	Y

WORDS TO FIND:

- [ ] Victory
- [ ] Royale
- [ ] Slurp
- [ ] Reboot
- [ ] Storm
- [ ] Sniper
- [ ] Fortnite
- [ ] Choppa
- [ ] Medkit
- [ ] Shield
- [ ] Chug Jug

ANSWERS ON PAGE 77.

SOLO TECHNIQUES

As a lone wolf, you need to rely on your skills, smart tactics, and game sense to outlast the competition. We've reviewed, tested and ranked several key strategies to help you secure that coveted Victory Royale.

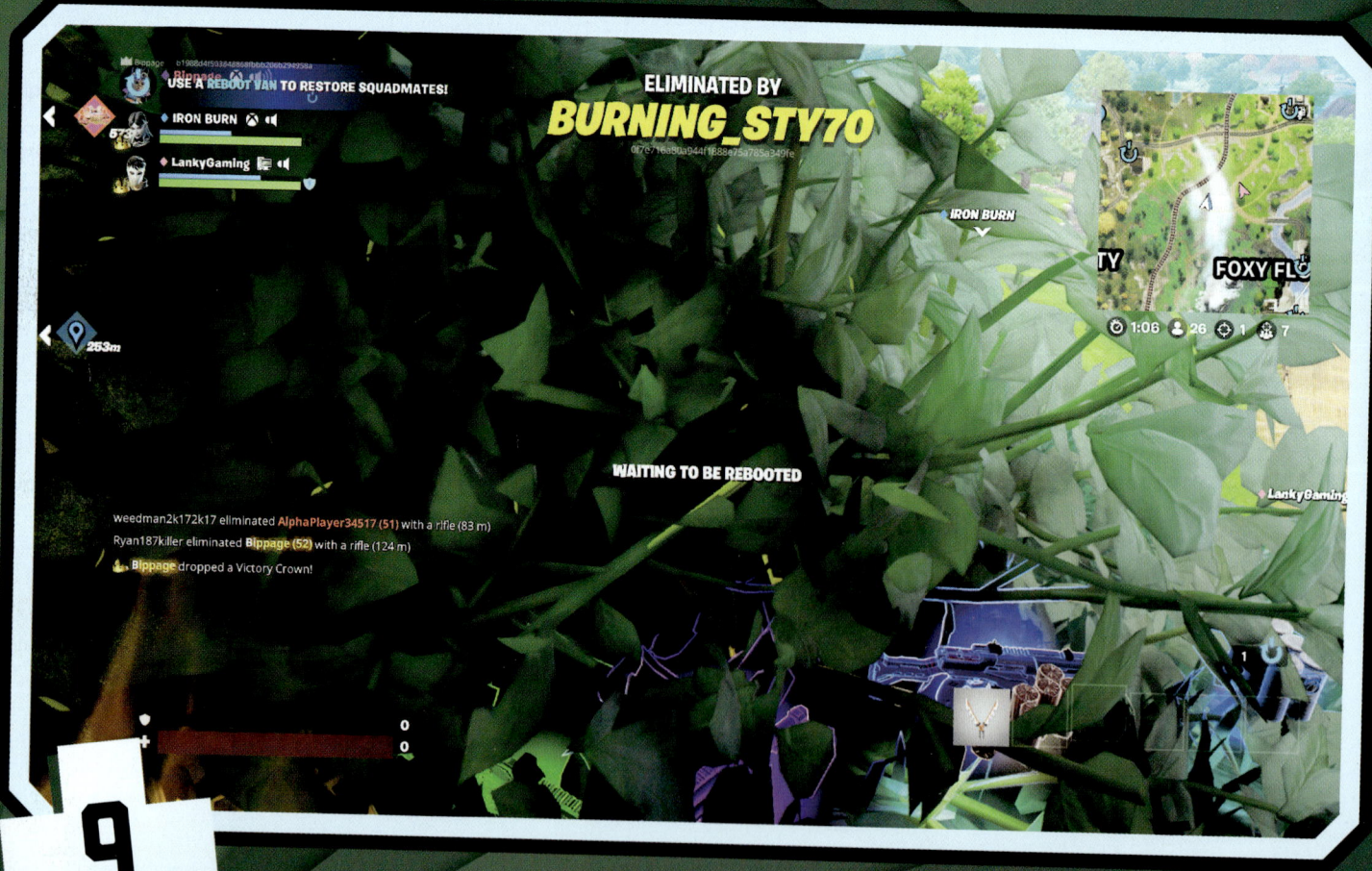

9
STAYING STEALTHY

Sometimes, discretion is the better part of valour. We find it useful to avoid drawing unnecessary attention by keeping a low profile early in the game. Use natural cover like trees, rocks and buildings to conceal your movements and wait for the right moment to strike or reposition.

BUILDING UNDER PRESSURE

In our opinion, building is a core skill that can turn the tide of a battle. Practise quick, efficient building to create cover, gain high ground, or block enemy shots. Even if you're under fire, a well-timed wall or ramp can save your life. Focus on developing your building speed through regular practise.

7

ROTATING AND POSITIONING

Smart rotations are crucial in solo play. Always be aware of the storm's movement and plan your path accordingly. Avoid predictable routes and use the terrain to your advantage. Good positioning can help you secure high ground, offer better visibility, and reduce your exposure to enemy fire.

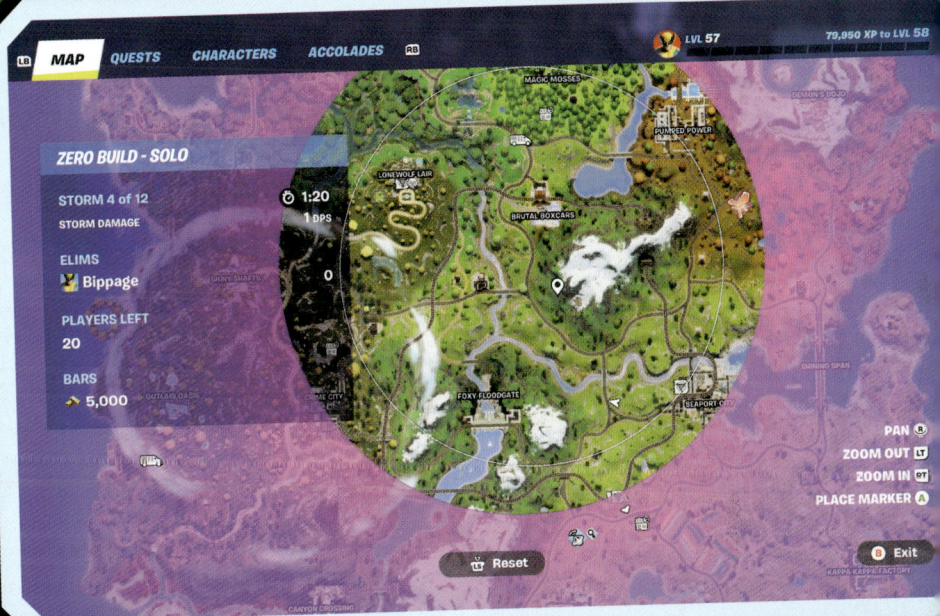

6

MANAGING RESOURCES

In a solo match, we think resource management can be a game changer. Ensure you have enough materials for building and keep your healing items handy. Constantly monitor your supplies and don't be afraid to change your plans if you're running low on essential resources.

5 WORKING WITH HIRES

In solo play, you might get a chance to hire NPCs for a temporary boost. These hired allies can distract enemies or provide extra firepower when you're in a tight spot. We think you should use them to cover your flanks or to force opponents to split their focus, but remember – they're here to support your own skills, not replace them.

4 KEEPING YOUR COOL

Solo matches can be intense and maintaining your composure is essential. Stay calm even when the pressure mounts and take a moment to plan your next move if you're caught in a tight spot. We think you'll find that a clear head leads to better decisions and ultimately, more wins.

3 ENGAGING WISELY

In solo mode, every engagement must be carefully considered. We suggest that you choose your battles rather than rushing into every fight. If you're low on health or outnumbered, it might be wiser to retreat and reposition rather than risk an unnecessary elimination.

2 OPTIMISING YOUR LOOT

Efficient looting is essential for solo play, in our book. Quickly gather essential items like weapons, shields and healing supplies. Prioritise finding a balanced loadout that suits both defence and offence. Remember, the right gear can be the difference between winning a firefight or retreating.

1 CHOOSING YOUR DROP ZONE

Your journey to victory starts before you even land. We advise picking a drop zone that suits your playstyle – a quieter area might let you gather loot without early confrontations, while a hotspot can offer quick action if you're confident in your combat skills.

GAMESWARRIOR VERDICT

Surviving solo isn't just about twitch reflexes – it's about strategy, awareness and staying cool under fire. We've found that mastering these basics, from smart rotations to quick builds, gives you a real edge when you're on your own. Put in the practise, stay sharp, and we're sure you'll be stacking up wins in no time.

SPEEDY WAYS TO BOOST YOUR XP

Fortnite is not only about fast-paced battles — it's also about smart strategies to rack up your XP and level up your gameplay. Whether you're a newbie or a seasoned player, knowing how to maximise your XP will help you unlock awesome rewards and new cosmetic items. We've tested out some of the more popular ways to boost XP quickly and these are the best approaches we've found.

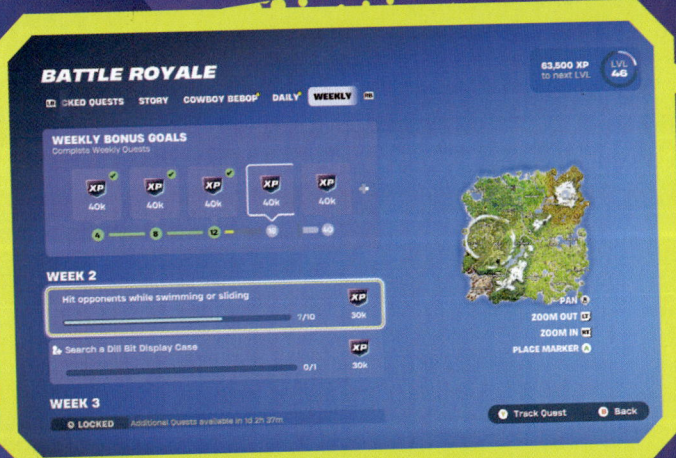

EMBRACE WEEKLY QUESTS

We say weekly quests are one of the best ways to earn a steady stream of XP. These challenges change every week, giving you fresh objectives and plenty of opportunities to earn rewards.

- **Variety and fun:** With different tasks every week, you get to try new gameplay tactics.
- **Consistent XP gains:** Completing these quests regularly adds up, giving you a significant XP boost over time.

GAMESWARRIOR XP BOOST FACTOR 9/10

TACKLE DAILY CHALLENGES

GAMESWARRIOR XP BOOST FACTOR 10/10

Daily challenges are a brilliant way to snag extra XP without the long grind. They're designed to be quick and engaging, which makes them perfect for a speedy XP boost in our opinion.

- **Check the requirements:** Before you jump into a match, have a quick look at your daily objectives.
- **Stay focused:** Completing a couple of daily tasks early in your session can set a winning pace.
- **Mix up your strategy:** Try different in-game approaches to keep the challenges exciting.

EXPLORE HIDDEN MAP SECRETS

Fortnite's map is full of surprises and exploring can be a rewarding XP adventure in itself. Look out for hidden areas and secret loot drops that sometimes come with bonus XP.

- **Secret Points of Interest (POIs):** Hidden bunkers and lesser-known landmarks might earn you extra XP.
- **Loot stashes:** Don't stick to the beaten path; you might find additional XP by exploring off-the-map areas.
- **Special in-game events:** Keep your eyes peeled for spontaneous events that offer bonus XP opportunities.

GAMESWARRIOR
XP BOOST FACTOR 7/10

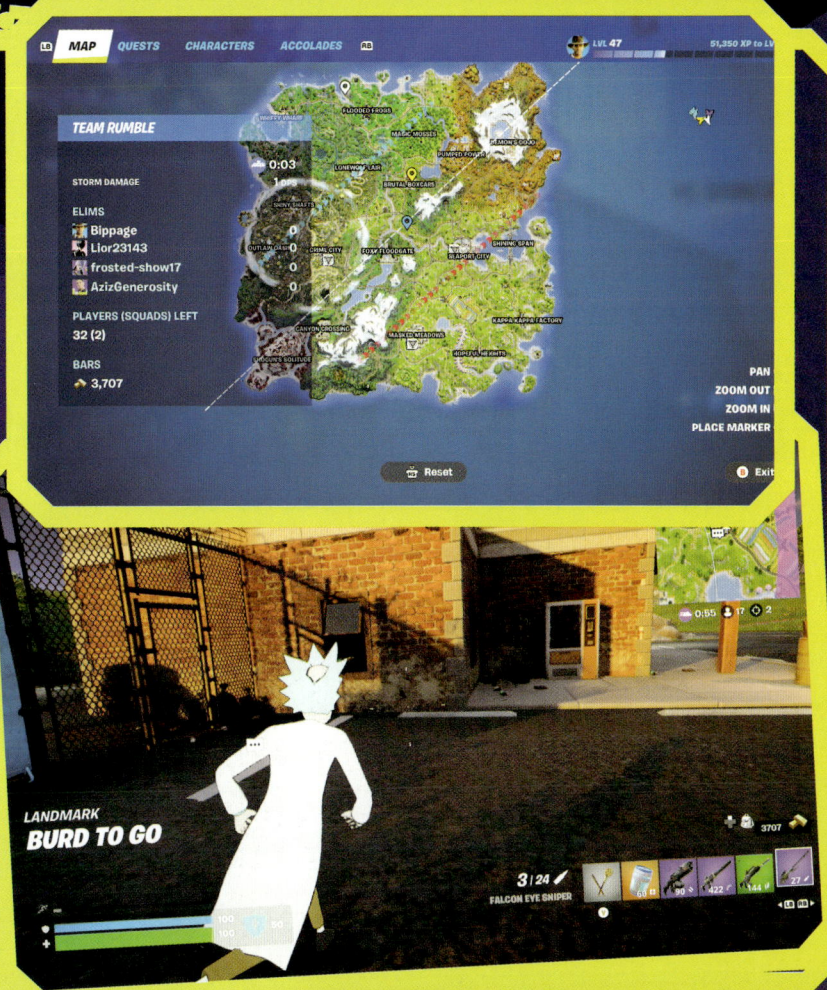

TEAM UP

GAMESWARRIOR
XP BOOST FACTOR 8/10

Playing with others isn't just more fun – we find it also helps you earn XP faster. Team-based challenges and coordinated strategies often lead to quicker, more effective completion of objectives.

- **Shared tactics:** Work together to overcome challenges and learn new strategies.
- **Motivational boost:** Friendly competition keeps everyone on their toes.
- **Collective XP:** Team up for challenges that reward group efforts and boost your overall XP gains.

TEAMWORK MAKES THE
DREAM WORK

Playing as part of a team is about working together, communicating, and using smart strategies to secure that Victory Royale. Whether you're new to squad play or already familiar with teaming up, there are plenty of ways to make your team unstoppable. We've reviewed the best approaches to teamwork and are sharing our favourites with you!

COMMUNICATING EFFECTIVELY

Good communication is the cornerstone of any successful team, in our opinion. Use your microphone or in-game commands to share vital information such as enemy locations, available loot and strategic plans. Clear, concise messages help avoid confusion during hectic firefights and ensure everyone knows their role.

GAMESWARRIOR
IMPORTANCE
RATING 9/10

CO-ORDINATING DROP ZONES

Before the match even begins, discuss where you want to land. Choosing a drop zone that suits your playstyle as a team is essential. Some areas offer plenty of loot but are more likely to see early conflict, while quieter zones might let you gear up safely. By co-ordinating your landing spot, you can avoid splitting up and ensure you're together from the start. We prefer quieter starts in squads so everyone can equip themselves for the adventure ahead!

GAMESWARRIOR IMPORTANCE RATING 10/10

SHARING LOOT AND RESOURCES

A good team always shares, in our opinion. Once you've landed and started looting, make sure to distribute valuable items among your teammates. If one person has a surplus of shields or medkits, pass some on to those who need it. Sharing means everyone has a better chance of surviving early encounters and later team battles.

GAMESWARRIOR IMPORTANCE RATING 8/10

USING GROUP HEALS EFFECTIVELY

Some healing items in Fortnite have the added bonus of healing more than just you – they can restore the health of your whole team. Items designed for group healing are incredibly useful in tight situations, which is why we love them. When you're all low on health, coordinate a time to use these items so that every team member benefits simultaneously.

GAMESWARRIOR IMPORTANCE RATING 8/10

SHARING AMMUNITION

Ammunition is a precious resource that can often be the difference between winning and losing a fight. Instead of hoarding ammo, make sure to pass extra magazines to teammates who might be running low. This not only helps keep the team in the fight longer but also prevents a situation where one player is overwhelmed due to a lack of firepower.

GAMESWARRIOR
IMPORTANCE RATING 7/10

A STRATEGIC APPROACH TO LOADOUTS AS A GROUP

We think that having a well-balanced team loadout is key to covering all your tactical bases. Discuss and decide on a loadout strategy before the match starts. For instance, one player could focus on close-range weapons like shotguns, while another specialises in long-range sniping. This way, you ensure that your team is prepared for every situation that might arise during the game.

GAMESWARRIOR
IMPORTANCE RATING 9/10

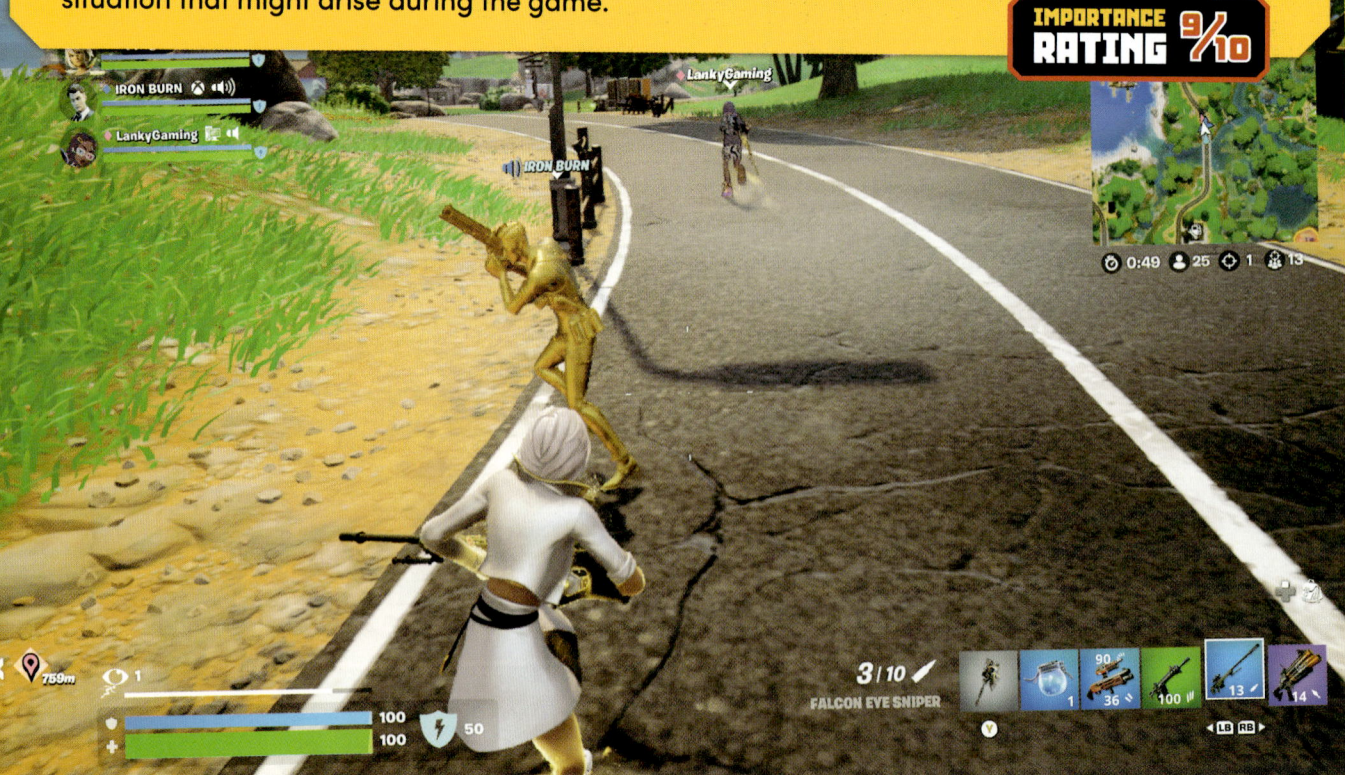

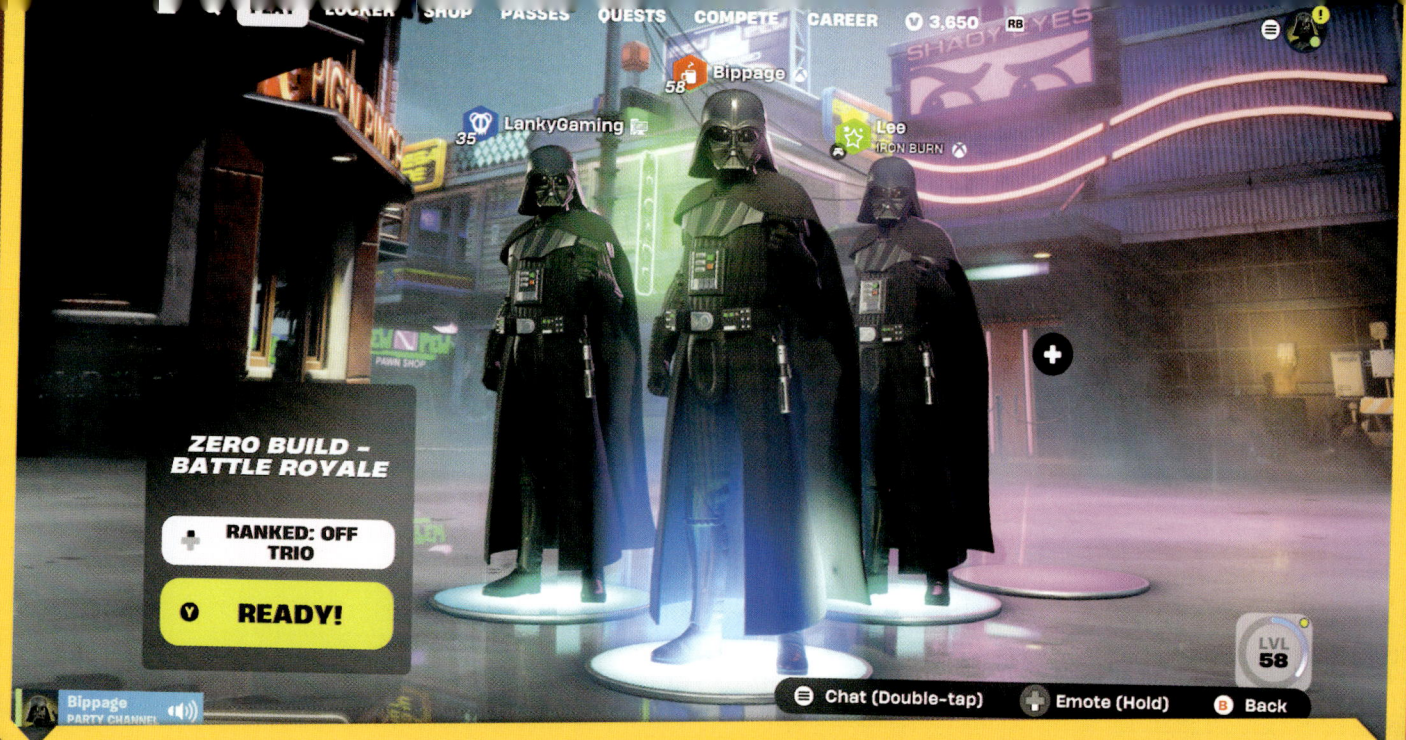

WEARING THE SAME OUTFIT TO CONFUSE OPPONENTS

This might sound a bit mad, but matching outfits can sometimes be a clever tactic. When every member of your team wears the same outfit, it can confuse opponents about who to target in the chaos of battle. We find opponents are more likely to hesitate or misidentify who is the most dangerous threat, giving your team a split-second advantage that can be vital during crucial moments.

GAMESWARRIOR IMPORTANCE RATING 7/10

CO-ORDINATED BUILDING STRATEGIES

Building is a critical skill in Fortnite and working together on structures can provide superior defence and tactical advantages. We suggest planning out building strategies during a firefight; for example, one teammate might focus on creating cover while another builds high ground. Co-ordinated building can help shield the team from fire and allow for better positioning when planning an attack or retreat.

GAMESWARRIOR IMPORTANCE RATING 7/10

SUPPORTING EACH OTHER IN COMBAT

In the heat of battle, it's essential to look out for one another. This means providing covering fire, reviving downed teammates and even distracting opponents so that a teammate can reposition. When you see a mate in trouble, act quickly to assist. This supportive approach can often be the turning point in a match, turning what could be a defeat into a victory.

ADAPTING STRATEGIES IN REAL TIME

No plan survives first contact and being adaptable is a crucial part of good teamwork. If your initial strategy isn't working, communicate with your team and adjust your tactics. Whether it's switching roles in response to enemy movements or retreating and regrouping, the ability to adapt quickly is a valuable skill that can keep your team one step ahead.

SHARING THE SPOTLIGHT

A strong team is built on trust and recognising that everyone has a role to play. Sometimes, we find it makes sense to let a teammate take the lead – whether it's for a coordinated attack or a crucial defensive move – as it can benefit the whole team. Don't be afraid to follow when someone else is making a strong play and be ready to step in with support when needed. Sharing the spotlight ensures that every member feels valued and contributes to the overall success.

GAMESWARRIOR IMPORTANCE RATING 9/10

CELEBRATING TEAMWORK AND LEARNING TOGETHER

Finally, always take a moment to celebrate your victories and learn from your defeats as a team. After each match, discuss what worked well and what could be improved. We find that constructive feedback can help everyone grow as players and build even stronger bonds for future matches. Remember, every game is an opportunity to refine your skills and learn from your teammates.

GAMESWARRIOR IMPORTANCE RATING 10/10

ZERO BUILD VS BATTLE ROYALE:

WHICH FORTNITE MODE SUITS YOU BEST?

Ever since Zero Build was introduced in Fortnite, players have been split. Some love the stripped-back simplicity, others stay loyal to traditional Battle Royale, with its frantic builds and sky-high towers. In our view, both modes offer something brilliant, but they definitely appeal to different playstyles.

GAMESWARRIOR SAYS

We've looked through the key differences that gamers have pointed out between the two styles, to guide you through the big differences. You can give each section a score out of 10 showing how important it is to you, then add up your score at the end to see which mode suits you best!

THE KEY DIFFERENCE

Let's start with the obvious: in Zero Build, you can't build. That means no last-second ramps to escape danger, no 1v1 towers and no boxing up mid-fight. Instead, Zero Build focuses more on movement, positioning and raw gunplay. In our opinion, it feels more like a traditional shooter.

Battle Royale, on the other hand, is all about building and editing. Matches tend to be faster-paced, with players who can build quickly often having the upper hand. For some, that's part of the thrill. For others, it's a barrier.

SCOREBOX

Zero Build   /10

Battle Royale   /10

SOLOS: SKILL VERSUS STRATEGY

In solos, Zero Build is all about awareness. You'll need to be clever with cover and movement. Outmanoeuvring an opponent by sliding, sprinting, or climbing can win you the fight. In our opinion, solos in Zero Build are tense and tactical – every sound matters.

In regular Battle Royale solos, the focus shifts to building skill. You'll often see players cranking builds to defend, escape or attack. If you're good at editing and reacting quickly, BR solos can be seriously rewarding.

SCOREBOX

| Zero Build | /10 |
| Battle Royale | /10 |

DUOS: TIGHT TEAMWORK

When playing in duos, communication is key in both modes, but the styles vary. In Zero Build, we find that teams succeed by sticking close, combining firepower and calling out movement. Holding high ground or sneaking around buildings often wins the day.

In Battle Royale duos, it's often about protecting each other while building. One player might build while the other heals. Fights are faster and more vertical, and a good duo can really shine by syncing builds and edits.

SCOREBOX

| Zero Build | /10 |
| Battle Royale | /10 |

TRIOS AND SQUADS: MAYHEM, BUT DIFFERENT KINDS

Squads are where the two modes really diverge. In Zero Build squads, it often becomes a full-on positioning game. We've seen matches won simply by smart rotations, good comms and using natural cover well. Third-party fights are more common, so squads that stick together tend to survive longer.

In Battle Royale squads, fights are louder, messier and faster. If even one teammate knows how to build under pressure, the team can hold off entire enemy squads. It's high-risk, high-reward stuff.

SCOREBOX

Zero Build	/10
Battle Royale	/10

MOVEMENT AND MOBILITY

Zero Build means thinking ahead is absolutely essential. It's far too easy to get stuck at the bottom of a cliff, leaving you vulnerable to attack from above or, even more annoyingly, being trapped there by the incoming storm.

In Battle Royale, you can be a little more flexible and reactive to your route through the game, safe in the knowledge that you can always build your way out of trouble should you find yourself in a sticky situation.

SCOREBOX

Zero Build	/10
Battle Royale	/10

LOADOUT PRIORITIES

Loadouts also shift depending on the mode. In Zero Build, we think accuracy-focused weapons and long-range gear shine – DMRs, Red-Eyes and grenades. Shield items and healing are also more important because you can't box up to heal.

In BR, shotguns and SMGs get more play because of close-quarters build fights. Players often carry at least one build-breaking weapon, like the Explosive Repeater, to take down structures.

SCOREBOX

Zero Build	/10
Battle Royale	/10

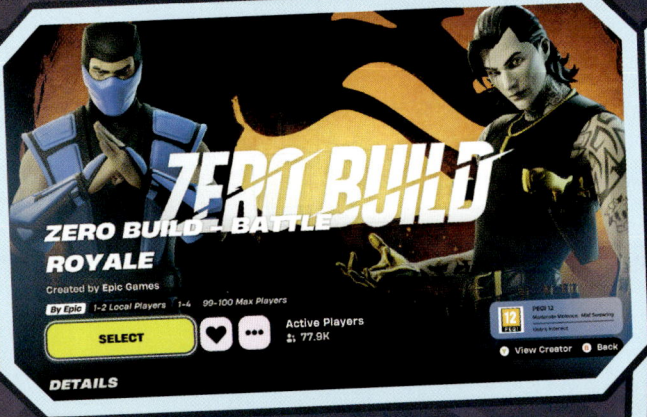

WHICH MODE IS HARDER?

Honestly, it depends who you ask. Some players say Zero Build is harder because there's no safety net. You can't build your way out of trouble. Others argue that Battle Royale takes more skill because of the learning curve involved in building and editing.

In our opinion, both modes offer a challenge. Zero Build tests your aim, movement and awareness. Battle Royale tests your speed, creativity and building under pressure. Both are hard in different ways – and that's what makes switching between them so fun.

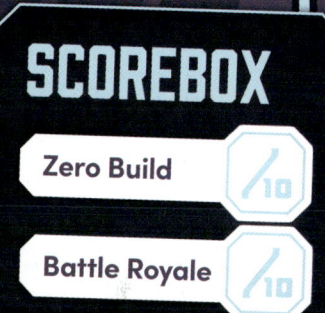

SCOREBOX

Zero Build	/10
Battle Royale	/10

WHICH MODE IS BEST FOR YOUR GAMESTYLE?

If you're all about fast fights, mechanical skill and creative plays, regular Battle Royale might be your thing. If you prefer tactical movement, smart positioning and sharp aim, Zero Build could be the better fit.

In our view, both modes are brilliant. The best way to decide? Try them both. See which one gets your heart racing. Or better yet – switch between them to keep things interesting.

Either way, grab your gear, thank the bus driver and drop in. Fortnite's got something for everyone.

SCOREBOX

Zero Build	/10
Battle Royale	/10

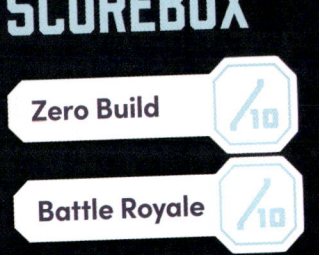

FINAL SCORECARD

Zero Build	/80
Battle Royale	/80

Add up your scores for each mode – **which one is best suited to you?**

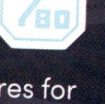

FORTNITE OG MODE: WHAT IT IS AND WHY IT'S BRILLIANT

The Fortnite OG game mode has quickly become a favourite with long-time players and curious newcomers alike. Whether you played Fortnite back in Chapter 1 or joined more recently, OG mode is a love letter to the early days of the game. It brings back classic weapons, locations and mechanics in a fast-paced, nostalgia-filled experience that feels both fresh and familiar. We've taken another look at the game now that it has reappeared as a permanent game mode, and we've reviewed what we feel are OG mode's best bits!

WHAT IS IT?

OG mode is a dedicated game mode that recreates the look, feel and features of Fortnite Chapter 1. In our view, it's the ultimate throwback. Players can return to iconic POIs like Tilted Towers, Retail Row, Pleasant Park and Dusty Depot, with a loot pool and visuals that reflect Fortnite's earliest seasons.

What makes it even better is that OG mode updates regularly to reflect different seasons from the original run. One week you could be racing ATKs across the desert in Season 5 and the next you're facing mechs in Season X. It keeps things exciting and ever-changing.

WHY PLAYERS LOVE IT

OG mode hits a nostalgic nerve for long-time fans who remember early Victory Royales, double-pumping shotguns and sneaky bush plays. For newer players, it's a chance to see where Fortnite began. In our opinion, it's a stripped-back version of the game that feels refreshing and fun in its simplicity.

FAST, FUN AND FULL OF ACTION

Matches in OG mode move quickly. We think you'll find that storm circles close faster, loot is easier to find and eliminations happen thick and fast. Every match feels action-packed and rarely drags. Even if you don't win, it's hard not to have fun.

CLASSIC WEAPONS ARE BACK

We think one of the best things about OG mode is the return of iconic gear. The Pump Shotgun, Tactical SMG, Heavy Sniper and classic SCAR all make a welcome return. For many players, these weapons are what Fortnite is all about.

SIMPLER MAP, SMARTER PLAYS

The OG map may look simpler, but it demands strategic thinking. With no vaults, mythics or NPCs, players rely on map knowledge, smart movement and strong building. POIs like Salty Springs and Greasy Grove feel familiar but still full of surprises.

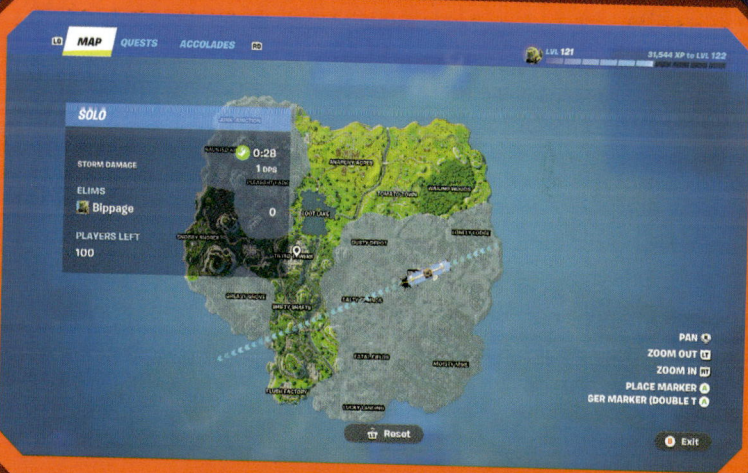

IT'S HERE TO STAY

OG mode started as a limited-time feature but is now part of Fortnite's permanent rotation. We think that's brilliant. It gives players a reliable, classic experience they can return to again and again.

MASTERING FORTNITE'S MOVEMENT:
BEYOND THE BASICS

Fortnite's evolution has brought more than just new weapons and locations; it's revolutionised how we move. Gone are the days of simple running and building. Now, we're talking about a parkour playground where mastering complicated moves can mean the difference between victory and a trip back to the lobby. We've rated some of the newer additions to the movement options and explained how we think they work best.

MANTLING

GAMESWARRIOR

COMPLEXITY FACTOR 2/5 | **USEFULNESS FACTOR 4/5**

Mantling is the foundation of modern Fortnite movement. It lets you grab onto ledges and pull yourself up, opening up countless new pathways. It's relatively simple to execute: just jump towards a ledge and hold the jump button. While straightforward, its usefulness is immense. It allows you to quickly gain height, escape enemies, or reach advantageous positions.

HURDLING

GAMESWARRIOR

COMPLEXITY FACTOR 3/5 | **USEFULNESS FACTOR 5/5**

Hurdling allows you to jump over an obstacle at the same level as you, or to pull yourself through a window. It's incredibly useful as it gives you another way into rooms that avoids the door, so you can surprise opponents who are holed up. However, you need to be looking at the ledge in order to hurdle properly – it's the only move that's frustratingly buggy and sometimes doesn't work so it can be a nightmare to pull off under pressure!

LEDGE JUMP

GAMESWARRIOR

COMPLEXITY FACTOR 3/5 | **USEFULNESS FACTOR 3/5**

The ledge jump adds a layer of finesse to your movement. When you're on a ledge, a well-timed jump can give you a small, but significant, boost. It's about timing and precision. You need to jump at the right moment to maximise the extra height. While not as flashy as other moves, it can be incredibly useful for reaching slightly higher platforms or escaping tight spots. The only downside to this move is that it takes a bit of practise to get the timing right.

ROLL LANDING

GAMESWARRIOR

COMPLEXITY FACTOR 2/5 | **USEFULNESS FACTOR** 3/5

Falling from great heights used to be a clunky affair. Now, with the roll landing, you can smoothly transition from a fall into a slide. This not only looks cool but also helps you maintain momentum and avoid that brief moment of vulnerability after a fall. To execute it, simply slide as you land. It's a simple mechanic, but it can make a big difference in maintaining speed and staying agile. It's especially useful when dropping from high structures or cliffs.

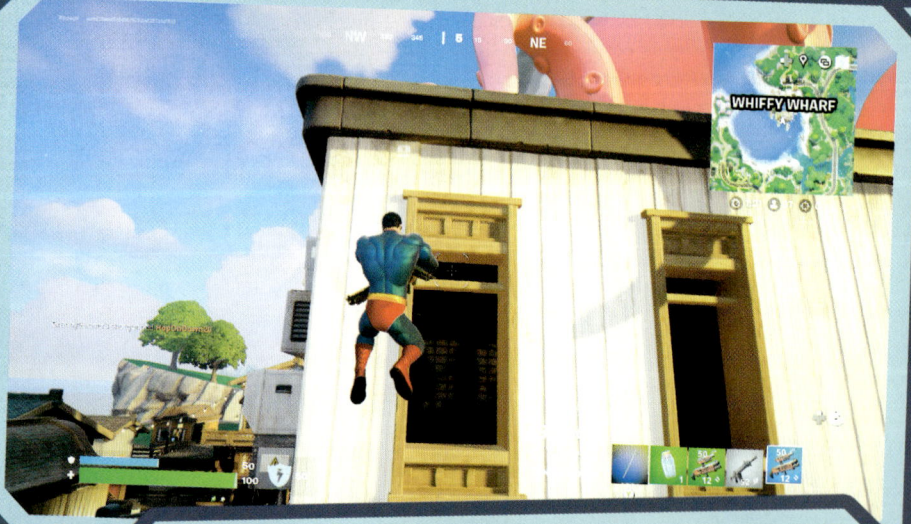

WALL KICK

GAMESWARRIOR

COMPLEXITY FACTOR 4/5 | **USEFULNESS FACTOR** 4/5

The wall kick is where things start to get a bit more complex. This move allows you to propel yourself off walls, giving you a burst of momentum. It requires precise timing and coordination. You need to jump towards a wall and then jump again as you make contact. It can be tricky to master, but the payoff is huge. It can be used to quickly change direction, gain height, or escape pursuing enemies. It's a very handy move but might take some time to master.

WALL SCRAMBLE

COMPLEXITY FACTOR 4/5 **USEFULNESS FACTOR** 5/5

The wall scramble enhances your climbing abilities, allowing you to scale walls more efficiently. This move is crucial for navigating vertical environments and reaching high vantage points. It involves a combination of mantling and jumping, allowing you to rapidly ascend walls. It requires a good understanding of timing and rhythm. It's challenging to master, but it opens up a whole new dimension of movement. In Zero Build, it's essential for getting the high ground.

SHOULDER BASHING

COMPLEXITY FACTOR 2/5 **USEFULNESS FACTOR** 4/5

Shoulder bashing lets you break through doors while sprinting or sliding. It's a quick and efficient way to enter buildings, especially when you're under pressure. To perform it, simply sprint or slide directly into a door. It's a straightforward move, but it can be incredibly useful for aggressive plays and quick escapes. It's a good way to catch opponents off guard and helps you keep your momentum while pushing.

STEPPING UP YOUR STYLE WITH KICKS

Introduced in November 2024, Fortnite Kicks are a **brand-new way** to customise your favourite outfits. These aren't just any shoes – they're a whole new category of cosmetic items, letting you swap out your character's default footwear for some *seriously stylish kicks!*

NIKE

Fortnite has partnered with some of the biggest names in footwear and Nike is definitely a highlight. You can find iconic styles like the Air Jordan 1, the Air Force 1, and the classic Cortez, all reimagined for the Fortnite world. These aren't just simple reskins, either. Many of the Nike Kicks feature incredible detail, with accurate colourways, textures and even subtle animations. Whether you're a sneakerhead in real life or just appreciate a bit of extra flair, the Nike collection is sure to have something to catch your eye.

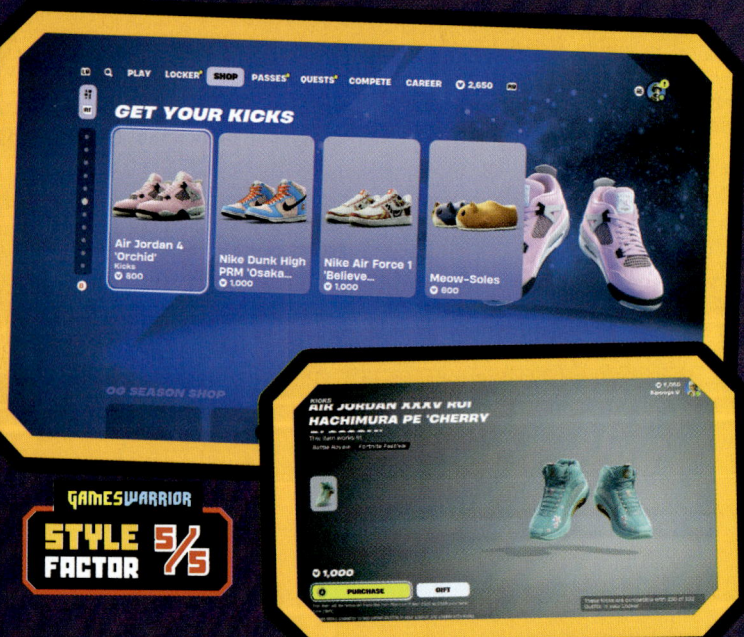

GAMESWARRIOR STYLE FACTOR 5/5

ADIDAS

For those who prefer the three stripes, Adidas also has a strong presence in the Item Shop. Expect to see classic silhouettes like the Superstar and the Stan Smith, along with some more futuristic designs. Adidas kicks often come in bold colourways and feature eye-catching details, making them a great way to stand out from the crowd.

GAMESWARRIOR STYLE FACTOR 4/5

CROCS

Believe it or not, even Crocs have made their way into Fortnite! These comfortable and undeniably unique shoes have become a cultural phenomenon and now you can rock them in-game too. From classic styles to more adventurous designs, the Fortnite Crocs collection offers a unique blend of comfort and personality.

GAMESWARRIOR
STYLE FACTOR 1/5

SILLY SHOES

Sometimes, you just want to have a bit of fun with your footwear. Luckily, Fortnite features a range of outlandish and whimsical shoe designs, from giant boots to fluffy slippers. If you're looking to add a touch of the unexpected to your Fortnite wardrobe, don't be afraid to explore the sillier styles on offer!

GAMESWARRIOR
STYLE FACTOR 2/5

FINDING THE PERFECT KICKS

Kicks can be found in the Item Shop, where they're regularly rotated in and out. You can also unlock them by completing Battle Pass quests. With new styles added all the time, there's always something fresh to discover. So, whether you're a sneaker enthusiast, a comfort-seeker, or just looking for a good laugh, there's a pair of Kicks out there for you.

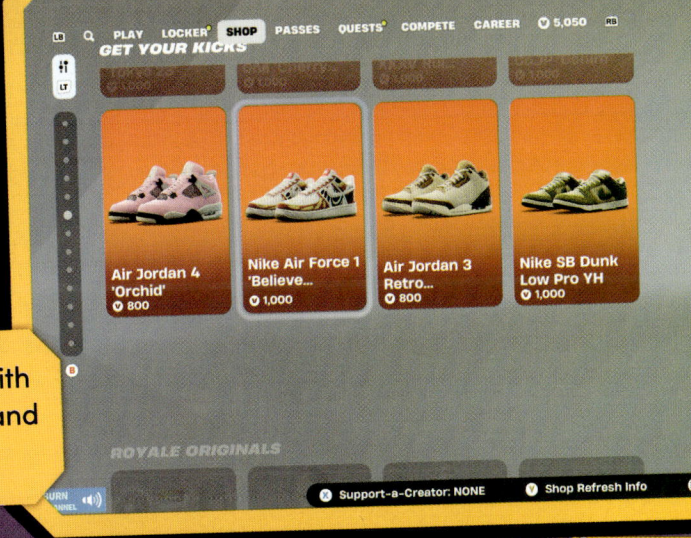

Important note: Not all Fortnite outfits are compatible with Kicks. However, Epic Games is constantly working to expand the compatibility list, so keep an eye out for updates.

TEN WAYS TO SURVIVE
THE FIRST CIRCLE IN FORTNIGHT

Fortnite's first circle is a whirlwind of chaos. As soon as you jump from the Battle Bus, you're thrust into a race for loot, cover and safety. We've assessed lots of different tactics to get through that first stage of the game and we've compiled a list of what we think are the best ten techniques to adopt.

1 CHOOSE YOUR LANDING SPOT WISELY

Your journey starts before you even land. Avoid overcrowded hot drops if you're after a quieter start. New POIs will always be very busy when they first appear, for example. Instead, target lesser-known spots on the map where you can loot peacefully. By landing in a quieter area, you give yourself time to gather essential supplies without constant fighting.

GAMESWARRIOR
IMPORTANCE RATING 5/5

2 GRAB ESSENTIAL WEAPONS FAST

In the early moments, your primary focus should be on arming yourself. Prioritise finding a reliable weapon, whether it's a shotgun for close-quarters brawls or an assault rifle for mid-range engagements. Even if you only find a basic pistol, having a weapon is better than nothing when a sudden scuffle breaks out.

GAMESWARRIOR
IMPORTANCE RATING 5/5

3 FARM MATERIALS EARLY

Building is one of Fortnite's most important mechanics. Right from the start, chop trees, break rocks and collect any materials you can. Aim for at least 200–300 materials so you're prepared to build defensive structures if an opponent surprises you.

GAMESWARRIOR IMPORTANCE RATING 3/5

4 KEEP MOVING AND STAY ON THE LOOKOUT

Staying still is a fast track to becoming an easy target. Once you've landed and collected some loot, keep moving from cover to cover. Jumping, sliding, or simply running from one safe spot to the next makes you a harder target for opponents who may be lurking nearby.

GAMESWARRIOR IMPORTANCE RATING 3/5

5 MANAGE YOUR HEALTH AND SHIELDS

Health and shields are your best friends early on. Grab shield potions, medkits, or Slurp Juices as soon as you can. If you're low on health, don't hesitate to use a medkit – being fully healed can be the difference between a narrow escape and a quick elimination.

GAMESWARRIOR IMPORTANCE RATING 5/5

6 LAND NEAR A HIRE

You're all alone when you land – so why not immediately double your chances? Consider landing at a location where an NPC is available for hire. This method does come with an element of risk, as locations with hires tend to make for a hot landing. However, if you practise landing at these spots, you should be able to land pretty much 'on' the hire and immediately recruit them – they will then provide covering fire and a distraction if you come under early attack!

GAMESWARRIOR
IMPORTANCE RATING 4/5

7 STAY AWARE OF THE STORM

The storm is always closing in and early in the game it might seem distant, but never ignore it. Keep an eye on the timer and the map and always have an idea of how to reach the next safe zone. This ensures you won't get caught off guard when the storm starts to bite.

GAMESWARRIOR
IMPORTANCE RATING 5/5

LOOT EFFICIENTLY AND PRIORITISE UPGRADES

When you're on the move, time is of the essence. Grab what you need quickly – don't waste too much time sorting your inventory in open areas. Prioritise picking up high-quality weapons and healing items. If you stumble across a Vault or a high-tier loot area, consider clearing it out to upgrade your arsenal.

GAMESWARRIOR IMPORTANCE RATING 3/5

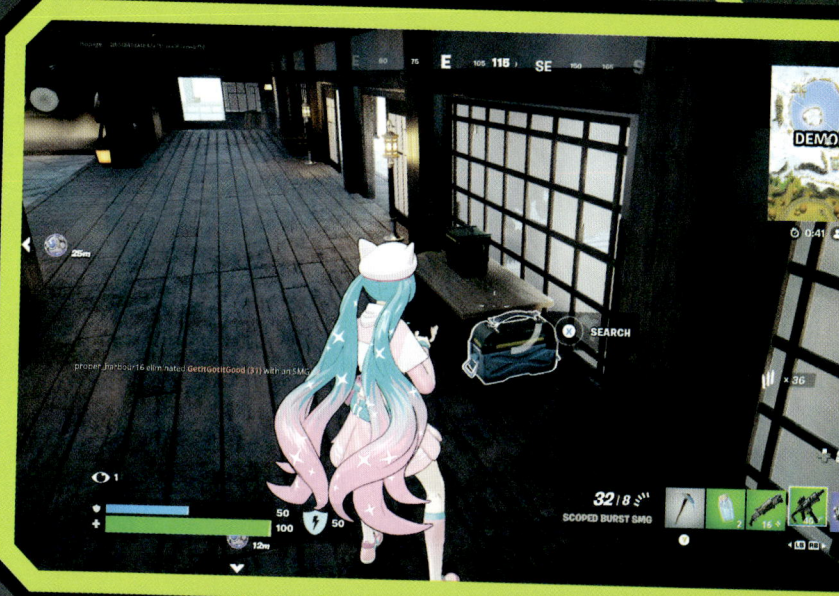

9 USE SOUND CUES TO STAY ALERT

Listening carefully can give you a significant advantage. Pay close attention to footsteps, gunfire, or even the sound of someone reloading. These audio cues can help you pinpoint nearby activity and avoid surprises. By tuning in to the sounds of the battlefield, you can adjust your route and strategy before danger comes too close.

GAMESWARRIOR IMPORTANCE RATING 4/5

10 KNOW WHEN TO FIGHT AND WHEN TO FLEE

Not every encounter is worth engaging. Early in the match, if you're low on health or lacking decent loot, it might be smarter to avoid a fight altogether. Sometimes, slipping away and repositioning can save you for later when the stakes are higher.
Remember: smart decision-making is key in Fortnite.

GAMESWARRIOR IMPORTANCE RATING 4/5

50 THINGS EVERY FORTNITE PLAYER SHOULD TRY (AT LEAST ONCE!)

Think you've done it all in Fortnite? Think again. From silly to sneaky, bold to just plain bizarre, we've put together our ultimate opinion list of 50 fun things every player should try at least once. Whether you're a **total noob** or a **seasoned sweat**, there's something here to shake up your next session.

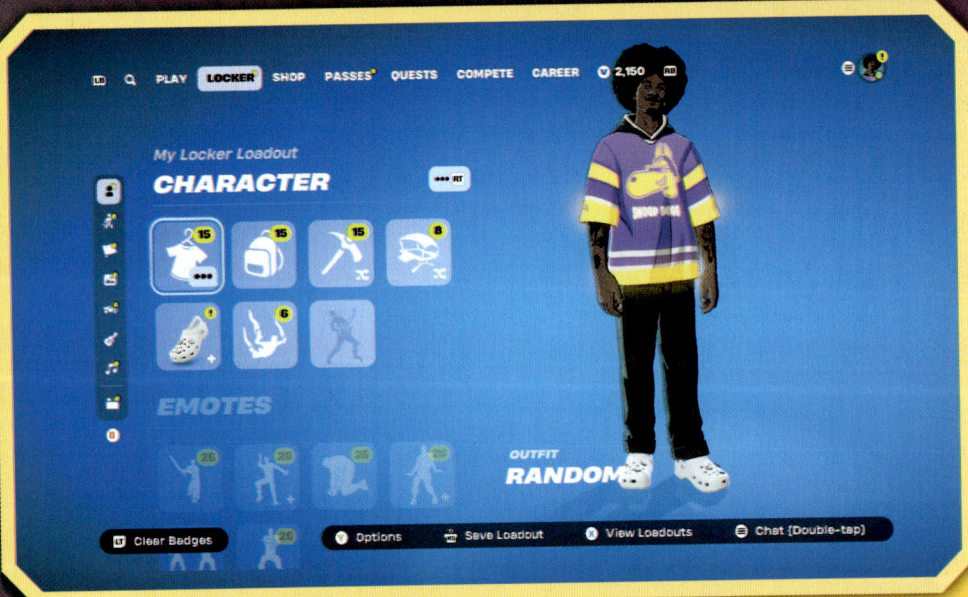

1

PLAY AS A CELEBRITY

Whatever you're into, there is a celebrity skin for you! Whether it's Neymar, Snoop or Ninja, using a celebrity avatar adds a real sense of fun to proceedings!

2

DANCE ON A CAR

You don't have to sit in a car – you can jump on the roof. Get a teammate to drive you round the map while you boogie away on the roof.

3

I CAN SEE YOU!

Use a flare gun, a scout NPC, a radar or another device to find opponents that you might not be able to see. Then you can sneak up on them and eliminate them!

4

ZIPWIRE ELIMINATION

While using a zipwire, pull your weapon and eliminate an opponent. You can flip reverse this achievement too – can you take out an opponent while THEY zipwire?

5

IT SMELLS IN THERE!

Hide in a dumpster until an opponent gets too close – then leap out and eliminate them!

6   FISHERMAN'S FRIEND

You've probably secured eliminations with most weapons – but can you do it with a fishing rod, hooking an opponent into the storm?

7   BUSH CAMP

Wearing camo gear is usually best for this one – can you camp in a bush and stay absolutely still when an opponent enters the bush? See if they leave without ever knowing you were there!

8

STORM CHASER

Kit yourself out with as many heals as you can find in the early stages of the game, then see how long you can survive in the storm. It's even possible to win this way!

9

NPC CARNAGE

Select an outfit that matches an NPC in the game, then land near them and see if you can fool other players into not attacking you – until you open fire yourself!

10 BACK YOU GO

See if you can use a Shockwave Grenade or a similar weapon to launch an opponent into the storm!

11 CATCH SOME SERIOUS AIR

How high can you go? Take a car or motorbike to the top of a mountain or cliff then speed off into the air – see how far you can travel!

12

GET AN ELIMINATION WITH A VEHICLE

There's no feeling quite like mowing down an unsuspecting opponent as you speed through the map! Line them up and knock them down – be aware you might need to go back to finish the job!

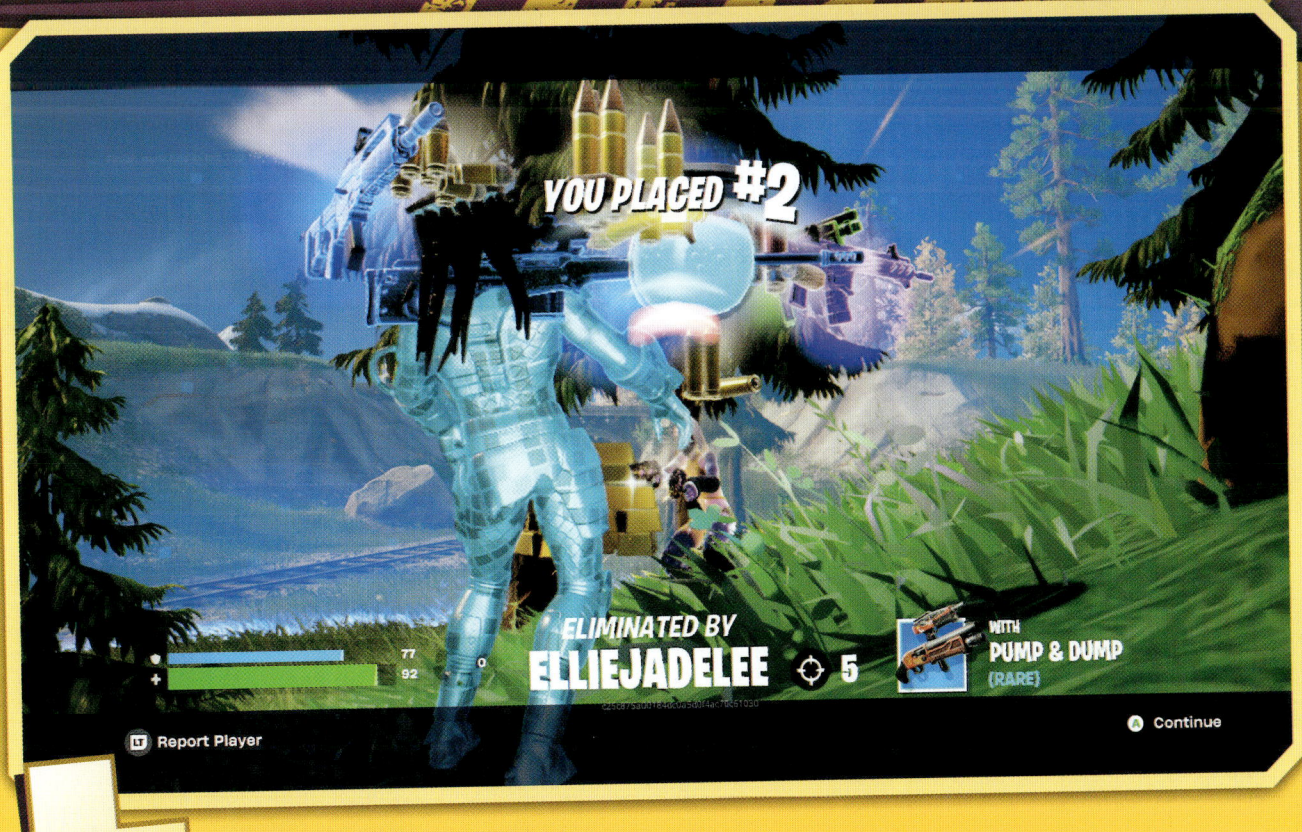

13

ONE MAN ARMY

Try playing duos, trios or even squads on no fill, so you're a team of one! How long can you survive?

14

SO NEAR AND YET SO FAR

Eliminate an opponent while they are at the reboot van trying to reboot a comrade. Two (or three, or even four) eliminations for the price of one!

15

TREETOP

Try hiding on top of a tree and see how many opponents you can eliminate before anyone spots you up there!

16

HITCH A RIDE WITH A RIVAL

If an opponent is trying to mow you down, spaming the 'enter vehicle' button with impact imminent can actually see you enter the passenger seat – and sometimes they won't even notice!

17 STAY IN THE CAR

Land near a vehicle and get into it as soon as you can. Then stay in the car for as long as possible, not leaving it for any reason! You'll need to refuel and probably repair your vehicle!

18 KING OF THE HILL

Land on the highest point of the map and stay there as long as possible, defending your high ground from your rivals and sniping into the distance!

19

SHOT OUT OF THE SKY

Can you eliminate an opponent while they are gliding to earth and finish them off before they've even landed?

20

SHOW OF PITY

When you're battling against another player, throw a heal item at them during combat. Bonus points awarded if they get to use it before you finish them off!

21

EXPLOSIVE FISHING

Instead of a fishing rod, use a grenade or another explosive to blow up a fishing spot and get all those lovely fish!

22

PROTECT THE PRESIDENT

Try playing a squads match where one of you has to remain unarmed and the others must all act as bodyguards, keeping the defenceless player safe for as long as possible.

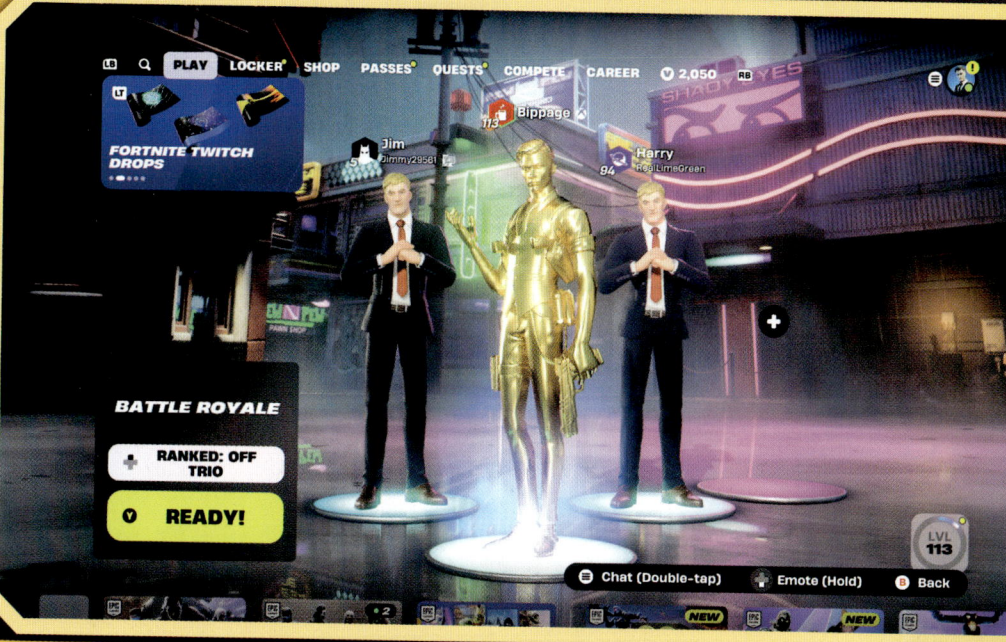

23

HOME RUN!

See if you can eliminate an opponent by knocking them off a high point on the map using a melee weapon.

24

THIRD PARTY WIN

Spy on two rivals having a shoot-out, wait for one to eliminate the other, then rush in to finish off the victor while they are still low on health and shield.

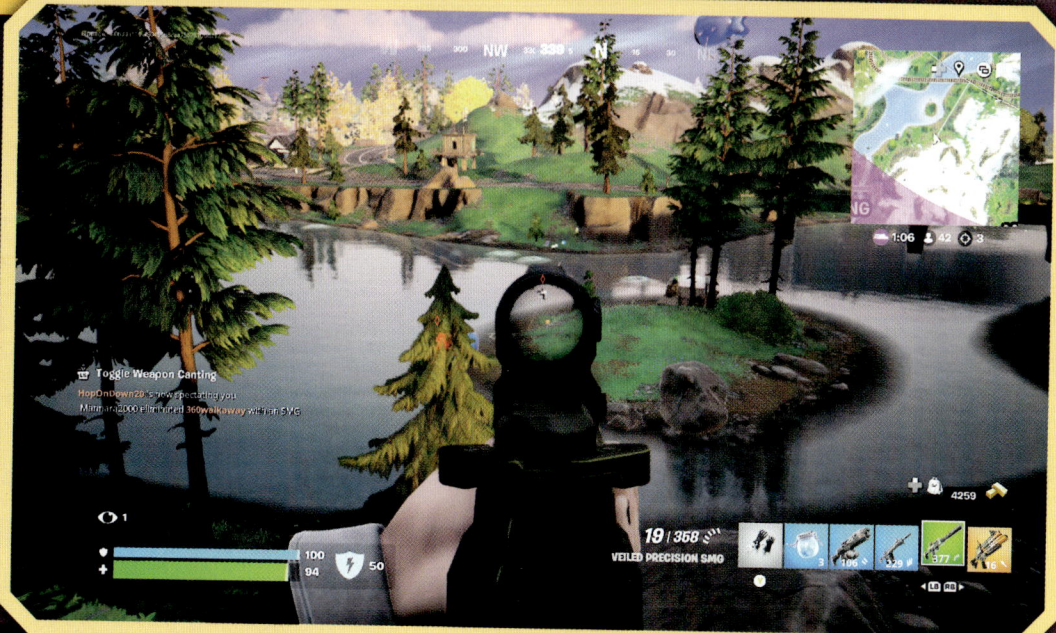

25

CUCKOO

If you're not much of a builder, take over someone else's construction after they have been defeated and use that as a solid base for your own building!

26

GOALS GALORE

There are often footy pitches placed on the Island – but did you know you get a celebration animation if you manage to kick the ball into the goal?

27

THIRD PARTY TROLLING

Sneak up on two opponents while they are battling and throw healing items at them so that the battle lasts longer – they'll be very confused by your help!

28 HIDE IN PLAIN SIGHT

Sit in the passenger seat of a vehicle and wait for an opponent to approach it before jumping out and opening fire!

29 I THINK YOU'LL FIND THAT'S MINE

Wait for another player to call in a supply drop, then take it for yourself – or wait for them to have opened it, then move in to eliminate them and nab the goodies!

30 BUILD ELIMINATION

Trap an opponent with a build that leaves them stuck in the storm – stopping them climbing a hill, for example, or blocking their only escape route!

31 FIRE IN THE HOLE

See if you can eliminate an opponent by setting fire to the structure they are in, or igniting the ground around them so they have no way of escaping!

32

MULTIBUNKER

Build a fort or similar construction by using at least 4 Port-A-Bunkers! Putting them on top of each other gives you a huge tower advantage in Zero Build!

33

MIDAS TOUCH

If you have the Midas skin, have fun creating chaos by discarding common weapons. Once you touch them they turn gold and other players can be fooled into thinking they are legendary or mythic weapons! If you don't have a Midas skin, keep an eye on the Item Shop!

34

BIG SPENDER

Save up all your gold until you max out and can't pick any more up – then blow the lot back to zero on goodies and hires, then start again!

35

MEDIC!

Play Team Rumble as a medic – you can't carry weapons, you can only carry heals that you give to other players so they last longer in combat. It can actually be a useful role to play!

36

CHALLENGE YOURSELF

Clear off all the challenges available to you – daily, weekly, storylines, the lot. As well as seeing more of the map, you'll get a boatload of XP!

37

BELIEVE AND ACHIEVE

Can you complete every accolade in the game? Check out the accolade screen in-game and focus on any you're missing – the feeling of contentment when you tick them all off is fantastic!

38

GAS STATION

Can you visit every single gas station on the Island in a single game? You'll need to be quick and hope that the storm circle is kind to you – but it can be done!

39

AIRBORNE DIVISION

Find two launch pads that are reasonably close to each other and just keep gliding from one to the other while you look out for opponents!

40

CARRY THE RAINBOW

Set yourself a colour challenge – can you collect one item of each colour so that your loadout looks like a rainbow?

41

CAR GO BOOM!

Unload your weapons into a vehicle carrying an opponent and see if you can explode their transport before they can escape – you might secure an elimination into the bargain!

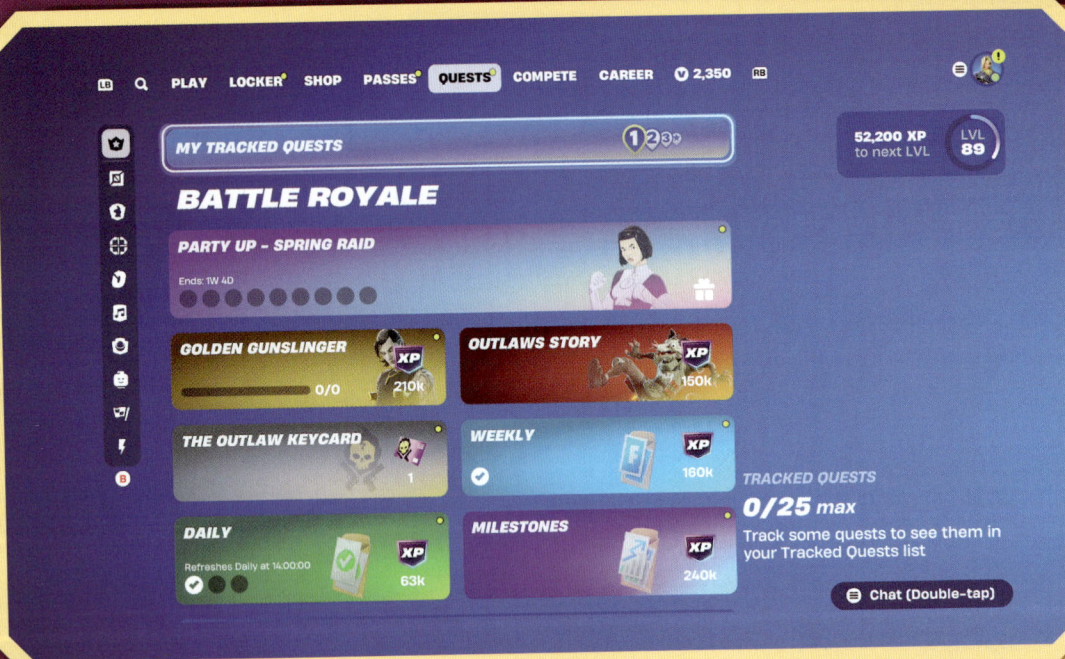

42

MEET AND GREET

Take time to visit every single NPC in the game so they're all unlocked. It can come in handy knowing who is where when you need to hire some extra help!

43

LOOT BAIT

Secure an elimination by hiding out near a big supply of loot, then eliminating any player that runs over to collect it!

44 DEFAULT GAMING

Playing a match using a default skin is always fun - in the heat of battle opponents can mistake you for a noob and you can take them by surprise with your battle skills!

45 LEGO OF REALITY

Give yourself a break from the mad crazy world of Fortnite by stepping into one of the excellent LEGO games that are now on offer. Most of your skins and items can be used too!

46

FEEL THE MUSIC

If music's your thing, give one of the musical experiences on Fortnite a go. We love Festival, where you can choose songs and tap along to the beat in time, using your controller. It's a relaxing alternative to Battle Royale!

47

ORIGINAL CONTENT

Spend some time exploring the many different mini games on offer that have been created by the brilliant Fortnite community. You're bound to find something you love and you can earn XP too!

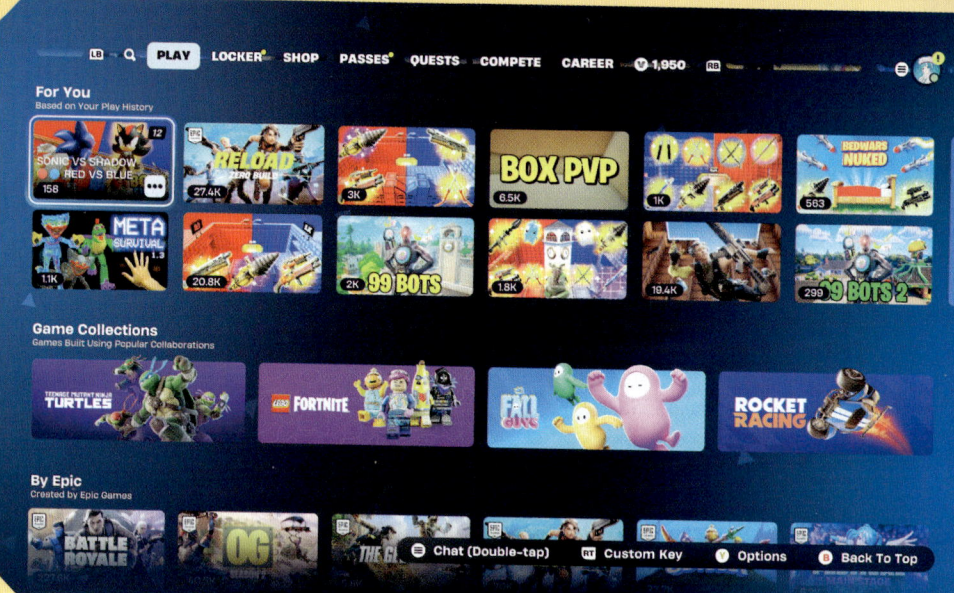

48

DO IT YOURSELF

Never mind playing games that other people have created – why not have a try at making your own Fortnite adventure? There are lots of different options and who knows – it might be the first step on route to becoming a games developer!

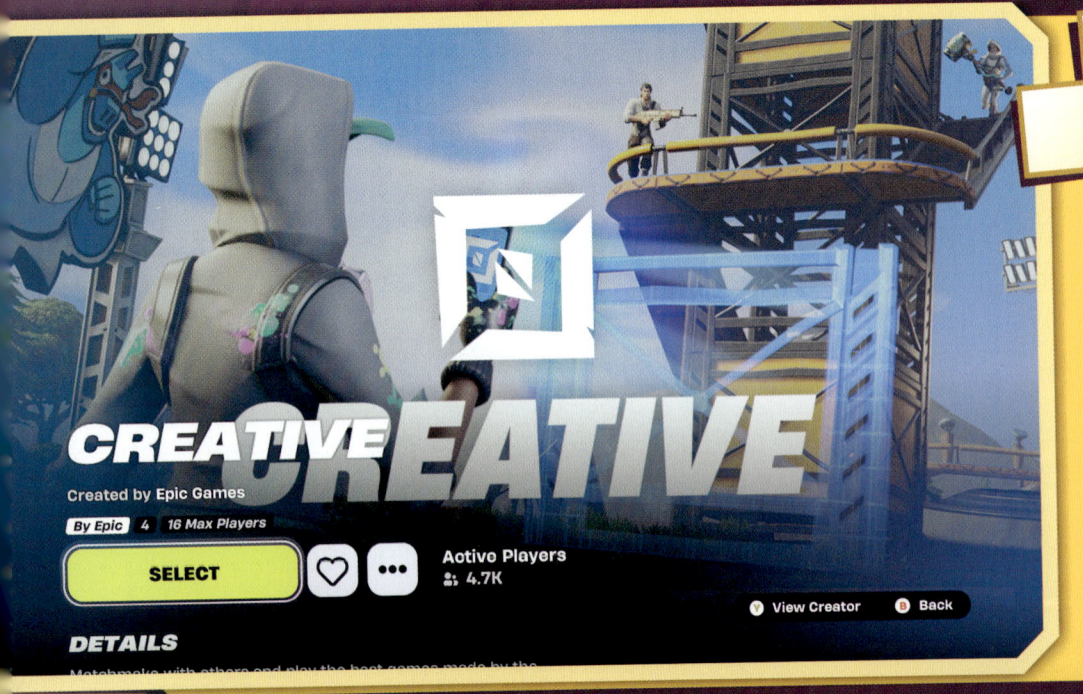

49 GRIND IT OUT

A fun challenge to set yourself is to find a suitably long rail on which to grind and to keep grinding back and forth on it for as long as you can - engaging with opponents is harder, but you're also tougher to hit! Can you secure some eliminations from your rail?

50 CATCH OF THE DAY

Time to kick back and forget all the gunfire and explosions. Grab yourself a fishing rod and enjoy the tranquility of fishing in the lakes and rivers around the Island.

GAMESWARRIOR VERDICT

We think this list proves there's more to Fortnite than chasing wins. We reviewed hundreds of different ways to make each session feel fresh and this top 50 list is bound to help you find new fun in Fortnite!

ICONIC FORTNITE SKINS RANKED!

Fortnite's locker room is **bursting with bizarre**, brilliant and downright legendary skins. We've rounded up 32 of the most iconic, scored them and given them a GamesWarrior ranking them from worst to first. **Let's go!**

32 YENNEFER OF VENGERBERG

| Fun | 2/5 | Originality | 3/5 |
| Style | 4/5 | Stealth | 3/5 |

We think Yennefer brings sleek, mystical elegance to the Island, but she's more a fan-service inclusion than a game-changer. Great for Witcher fans, less so for standout moments.

31 X-23

| Fun | 3/5 | Originality | 3/5 |
| Style | 4/5 | Stealth | 4/5 |

A sharp choice (literally), but X-23 doesn't quite claw her way into Fortnite greatness. We like the comic authenticity, though she lacks that over-the-top flair.

30 WONDER WOMAN

| Fun | 2/5 | Originality | 2/5 |
| Style | 3/5 | Stealth | 2/5 |

We expected more. Iconic, sure, but Wonder Woman feels like a slightly reskinned default. Not enough pizzazz to compete with Fortnite's flashier legends.

29 WEAPON X

Fun	3/5
Originality	3/5
Style	3/5
Stealth	4/5

Logan's more feral form looks mean, but doesn't quite stand out. Great for lurking in shadows, less exciting when standing still in the locker.

OUTFIT
WEAPON X

These items may work in:
Battle Royale   Fortnite Festival   Rocket Racing
LEGO® Fortnite Odyssey   LEGO® Fortnite Brick Life

550 · Bippage

2,000

GET V-BUCKS   GIFT

This item will be removed from the Item Shop on 12 Apr 2025 at 00:59 your local time (GMT+1).

These cosmetic items grant no competitive advantage. Outfits and wraps don't include weapons. Not all cosmetics are usable in all experiences. For more details on cosmetic variations and limitations of use, see fn.gg/cosmetics

Back

OUTFIT
UNDERTAKER

This item works in:
Battle Royale   Fortnite Festival   Rocket Racing

850 · Bippage

1,500

GET V-BUCKS   GIFT

Part of the Undertaker & Cody Rhodes Bundle

VIEW BUNDLE

This item will be removed from the Item Shop on 24 Apr 2025 at 00:59 your local time (GMT+1).

These cosmetic items grant no competitive advantage. Outfits and wraps don't include weapons. Not all cosmetics are usable in all experiences. For more details on cosmetic variations and limitations of use, see fn.gg/cosmetics

Back

28 THE UNDERTAKER

Fun	3/5
Originality	2/5
Style	3/5
Stealth	4/5

A wrestling legend in Fortnite form, but we feel The Undertaker belongs more in a ring than a battle bus. Grim? Yes. Memorable? Not quite.

---

27 THE INCREDIBLES

Fun	4/5
Originality	2/5
Style	3/5
Stealth	2/5

They're literally incredible, but the translation to Fortnite feels just OK. Nostalgic and fun, but not the kind of family to carry a win.

3,700 V-BUCKS OFF

BUNDLE
THE INCREDIBLE BUNDLE

These items may work in:
Battle Royale   Fortnite Festival   Rocket Racing
LEGO® Fortnite

4,0... · Bippage

The price for included items is:
3,500   7,200

PURCHASE   GIFT

This item will be removed from the Item Shop on 10/8/24 at 12:59 AM your local time (GMT+1).

These cosmetic items grant no competitive advantage. Outfits and wraps don't include weapons. Not all cosmetics are usable in all experiences. For more details on cosmetic variations and limitations of use, see fn.gg/cosmetics

Camera

ICON SERIES   OUTFIT – FORTNITE STYLE
SNOOP DOGG

This item works in:
Battle Royale   Fortnite Festival   Rocket Racing

S-N-Double O-P D-O-Double G.
Part of the Snoop Dogg set.
Introduced in Chapter Fortnite: Remix, Season Fortnite: Remix.
[Transformation], [Selectable Styles]

STYLE (SNOOP DOGG)

THE DOGG (OFF)

GLASSES (SQUARE GLASSES)

All styles shown here are included with purchase and can be changed at any time in the Locker.

Camera

26 SNOOP DOGG

Fun	4/5
Originality	4/5
Style	4/5
Stealth	1/5

A style icon with charisma to spare, but subtlety isn't Snoop's strong suit. We love him, but he's more party than pro play.

25 SKIBIDI TOILET

| Fun | 5/5 | Originality | 5/5 |
| Style | 2/5 | Stealth | 1/5 |

The bizarre internet chaos we didn't ask for but secretly enjoy. Outrageous and meme-heavy. You won't win many games, but you'll get noticed.

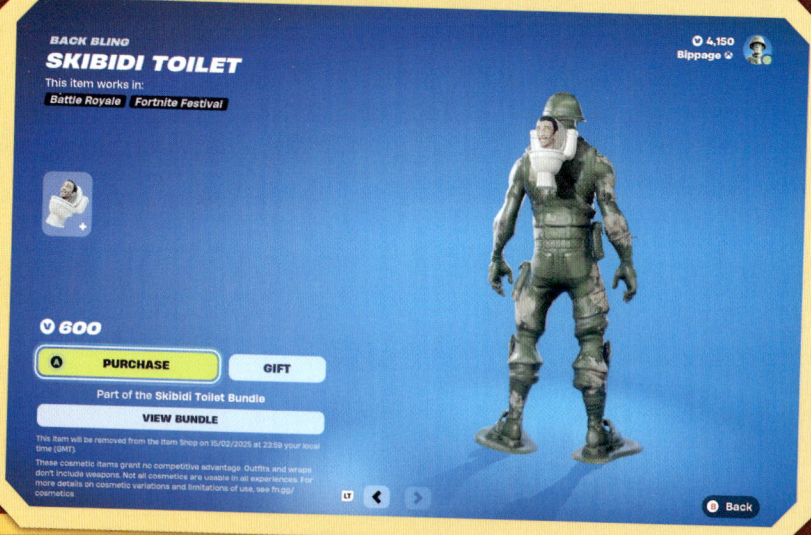

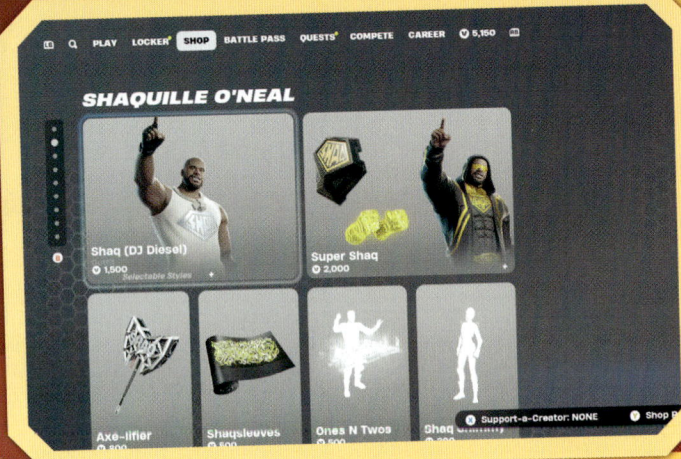

24 SHAQ

| Fun | 4/5 | Originality | 3/5 |
| Style | 4/5 | Stealth | 1/5 |

It's Shaq. He's massive, impossible to miss, and surprisingly fun to run around with. Not ideal for stealthy play, but brilliant for dunks.

23 RYOMEN SUKUNA

| Fun | 3/5 | Originality | 4/5 |
| Style | 5/5 | Stealth | 3/5 |

Anime menace with serious drip. Ryomen feels fresh, powerful and dangerous. We think he deserves more attention than he gets.

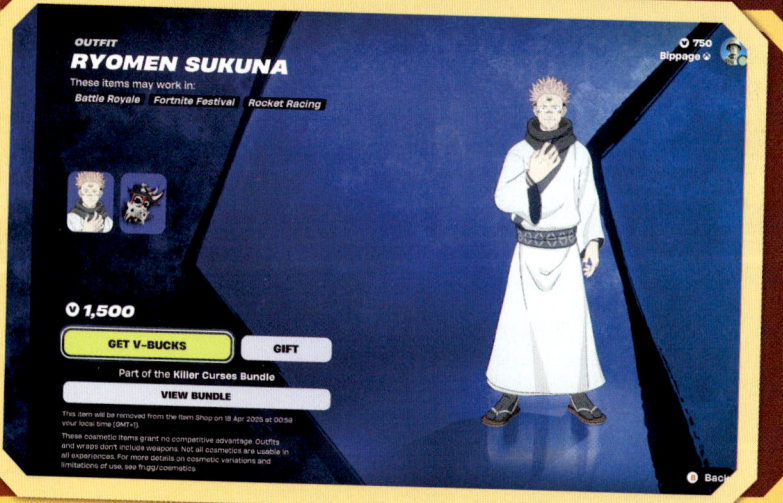

22 PAULIE FEATHERFACE

| Fun | 4/5 | Originality | 5/5 |
| Style | 3/5 | Stealth | 2/5 |

Half ridiculous, half genius. Featherface is a walking contradiction and somehow it works. Points for originality, even if he's an easy target.

21 NIKE GODDESS

Fun	3/5	Originality	3/5
Style	5/5	Stealth	3/5

Myth meets modern branding in this elegant crossover. Nike Goddess is a vibe and we can't deny she looks fantastic gliding into the storm.

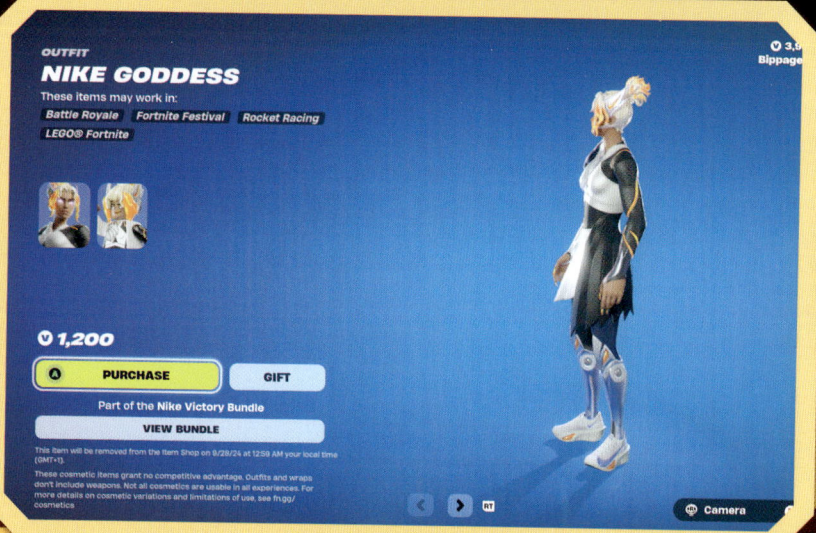

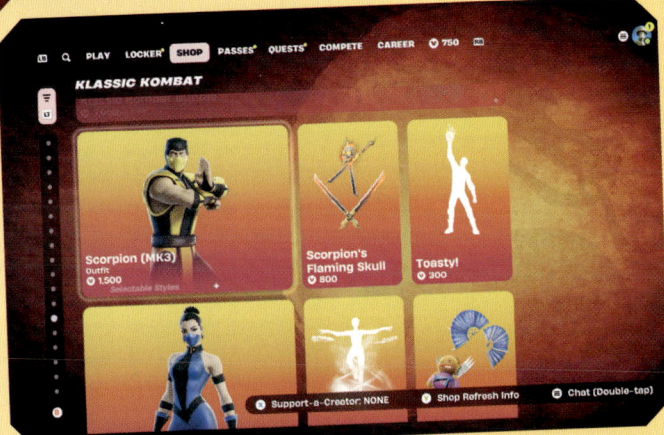

20 MORTAL KOMBAT

Fun	5/5	Originality	2/5
Style	4/5	Stealth	3/5

Finishing moves would've been cooler, but the skin still kicks hard. Familiar but fierce, Mortal Kombat brings that retro brutality.

19 MECHA MORTY

Fun	4/5	Originality	4/5
Style	3/5	Stealth	2/5

Rick gets all the love, but Mecha Morty is an underrated gem. A weird and wonderful piece of crossover chaos.

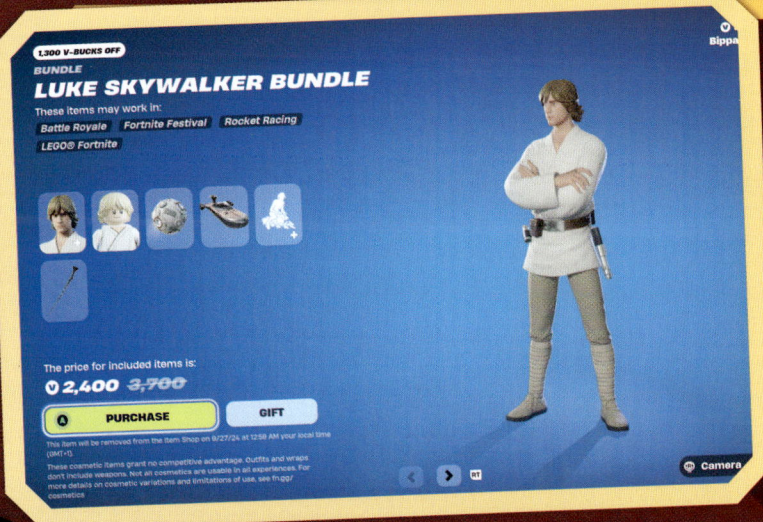

18 LUKE SKYWALKER

Fun	3/5	Originality	3/5
Style	4/5	Stealth	3/5

Classic Jedi cool, but maybe a bit too safe. Luke blends in a little too well, but his legacy still lands.

17

KRANG'S ANDROID

Fun	4/5	Originality	5/5
Style	3/5	Stealth	2/5

This one's wild. A giant torso with a brain in its stomach? Count us in. Weird, nostalgic and exactly the kind of oddball we love in Fortnite.

OUTFIT – FORTNITE STYLE
KRANG'S ANDROID
This item works in:
Battle Royale   Fortnite Festival   Rocket Racing

An android body built by Krang and Shredder equipped with weaponry. Part of the **TMNT** set.
Introduced in **Chapter 6, Season 2**.
[Built-in]

⚡ 850
Bippage

Dimension Axe shows a different style when equipped with Krang's Android outfit!

Camera   Back

OUTFIT
KONG
These items may work in:
Battle Royale   Fortnite Festival   Rocket Racing

⚡ 2,950
Bippage

⚡ 1,500
PURCHASE   GIFT
Part of the Mechagodzilla & Kong Bundle
VIEW BUNDLE

This item will be removed from the Item Shop on 24/01/2025 at 2359 your local time (GMT).
These cosmetic items grant no competitive advantage. Outfits and wraps don't include weapons. Not all cosmetics are usable in all experiences. For more details on cosmetic variations and limitations of use, see fn.gg/cosmetics

Back

16

KONG

Fun	4/5	Originality	3/5
Style	4/5	Stealth	2/5

Massive, menacing and weirdly majestic, Kong stomps his way up the list. Not subtle by any means, but loads of fun if you enjoy being a target.

15

JOHN WICK

Fun	4/5	Originality	3/5
Style	5/5	Stealth	4/5

Slick and deadly, John Wick is a classic for a reason. He oozes cool and you'll feel invincible... until someone dances on you.

OUTFIT
JOHN WICK
These items may work in:
Battle Royale   Fortnite Festival   Rocket Racing

⚡ 850
Bippage

1 of 4

⚡ 2,000
GET V-BUCKS   GIFT
Part of the John Wick Bundle
VIEW BUNDLE

This item will be removed from the Item Shop on 28 Apr 2025 at 0059 your local time (GMT+1).
These cosmetic items grant no competitive advantage. Outfits and wraps don't include weapons. Not all cosmetics are usable in all experiences. For more details on cosmetic variations and limitations of use, see fn.gg/cosmetics

Back

OUTFIT
THE GIANT CHICKEN
These items may work in:
Battle Royale   Fortnite Festival   Rocket Racing

⚡ 3,150
Bippage

⚡ 1,500
PURCHASE   GIFT
Part of the The Giant Chicken Bundle
VIEW BUNDLE

This item will be removed from the Item Shop on 26/01/2025 at 2359 your local time (GMT).
These cosmetic items grant no competitive advantage. Outfits and wraps don't include weapons. Not all cosmetics are usable in all experiences. For more details on cosmetic variations and limitations of use, see fn.gg/cosmetics

Back

14

THE GIANT CHICKEN

Fun	5/5	Originality	5/5
Style	2/5	Stealth	1/5

Absurd? Yes. Effective? Occasionally. The Giant Chicken might not win beauty contests, but it's hard not to smile while pecking around the map.

13 GHOST RI-DURRR

Fun	4/5	Originality	4/5
Style	5/5	Stealth	2/5

This blazing biker burns bright in any match. Not the sneakiest skin, but certainly one of the coolest to ride into battle.

12 GAGA

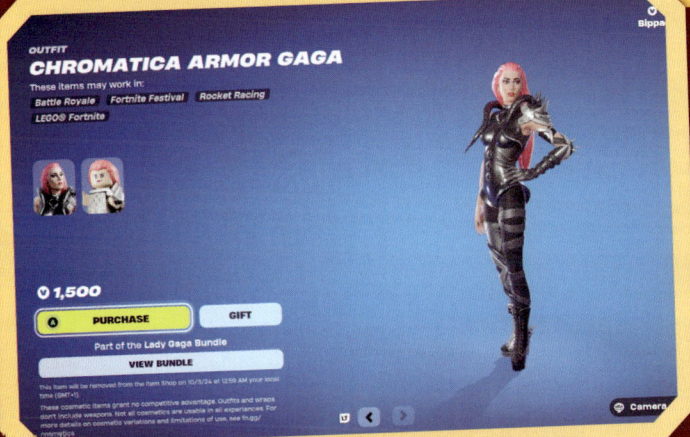

Fun	4/5	Originality	5/5
Style	5/5	Stealth	1/5

Fashion-forward and full of flair, Gaga brings theatre to Fortnite. Definitely not one for lurking in bushes, but unmatched for flair.

11 FISHSTICK

Fun	5/5	Originality	5/5
Style	3/5	Stealth	2/5

An iconic meme skin turned Fortnite legend. Fishstick has personality for days and is always a crowd-pleaser, even if he's rarely the last one standing.

10 EDWARD SCISSORHANDS

Fun	4/5	Originality	4/5
Style	5/5	Stealth	2/5

A gothic icon with style to spare. Edward's delicate edge is hauntingly beautiful and we think he's earned his spot near the top.

9 CHLOE KIM

Fun	4/5	Originality	4/5
Style	4/5	Stealth	3/5

Balanced, bold and surprisingly fun to play as. Chloe might not shout the loudest, but her cool confidence carries.

OUTFIT
CHLOE KIM
These items may work in:
Battle Royale · Fortnite Festival · Rocket Racing
LEGO® Fortnite Odyssey · LEGO® Fortnite Brick Life

🪙 1,500

PURCHASE · **GIFT**

Part of the Chloe Kim Bundle

VIEW BUNDLE

With the reactive Deep Freeze style, ices over with eliminations!

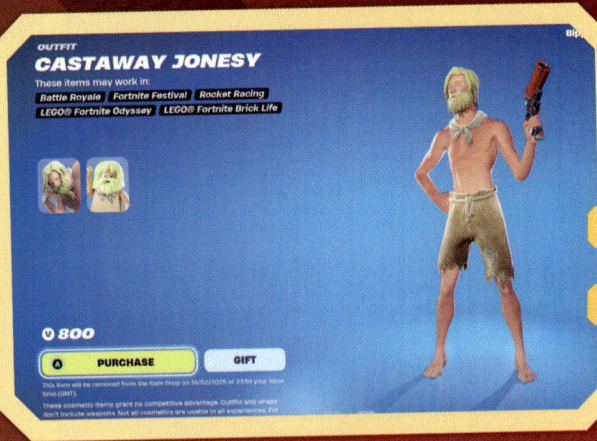

OUTFIT
CASTAWAY JONESY
These items may work in:
Battle Royale · Fortnite Festival · Rocket Racing
LEGO® Fortnite Odyssey · LEGO® Fortnite Brick Life

🪙 800

PURCHASE · **GIFT**

8 CASTAWAY JONESY

Fun	5/5	Originality	4/5
Style	3/5	Stealth	4/5

The survivalist king of casual cool. We think Castaway Jonesy deserves cult status – simple, scrappy and strangely satisfying to use.

---

7 BILLIE EILISH

Fun	5/5	Originality	4/5
Style	5/5	Stealth	3/5

Dark pop power in digital form. Billie's moody aesthetic is a standout in the locker, and she somehow feels both low-key and high impact.

OUTFIT
RED ROOTS BILLIE
These items may work in:
Battle Royale · Fortnite Festival · Rocket Racing
LEGO® Fortnite Odyssey · LEGO® Fortnite Brick Life

🪙 1,500

GET V-BUCKS · **GIFT**

Part of the Billie Eilish Bundle

VIEW BUNDLE

OUTFIT
BIANCA BELAIR
These items may work in:
Battle Royale · Fortnite Festival · Rocket Racing

🪙 1,500

GET V-BUCKS · **GIFT**

Part of the Becky Lynch & Bianca Belair Bundle

VIEW BUNDLE

6 BIANCA BELAIR

Fun	5/5	Originality	4/5
Style	5/5	Stealth	2/5

She's the 'EST' of Fortnite now too. Bianca brings fierce energy and flair, and we think she's a perfect pick for confident players.

---

5 BATMAN ZERO

Fun	4/5	Originality	3/5
Style	5/5	Stealth	4/5

Dark, brooding and battle-ready. Batman Zero feels like a true tactician's choice. Tactical cape? Tick. Grit? Double tick.

BUNDLE
BATMAN ZERO BUNDLE
These items may work in:
Battle Royale · Fortnite Festival · Rocket Racing
LEGO® Fortnite Odyssey · LEGO® Fortnite Brick Life

The price for included items is:
🪙 2,100 ~~3,500~~

PURCHASE · **GIFT**

Loading Screen Included!

4

ARIANA GRANDE

Fun	5/5	**Originality**	5/5
Style	5/5	**Stealth**	2/5

A high-fashion diva meets cosmic queen. Ariana's skin is stunning, sparkling and surreal. If we could give extra points for vibes, she'd win outright.

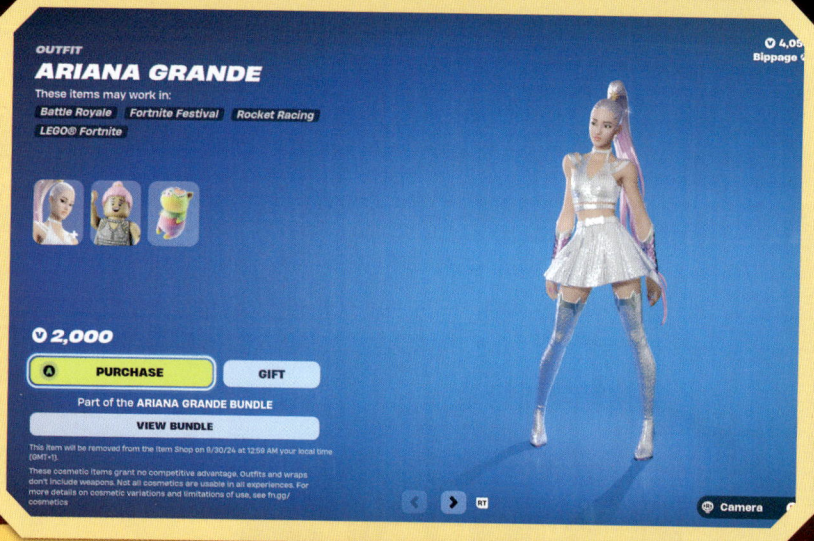

OUTFIT
ARIANA GRANDE
These items may work in:
Battle Royale | Fortnite Festival | Rocket Racing
LEGO® Fortnite

2,000

PURCHASE | GIFT

Part of the **ARIANA GRANDE BUNDLE**

VIEW BUNDLE

OUTFIT
ANDERSON .PAAK
These items may work in:
Battle Royale | Fortnite Festival | Rocket Racing
LEGO® Fortnite

1,500

PURCHASE | GIFT

3

ANDERSON .PAAK

Fun	5/5	**Originality**	5/5
Style	5/5	**Stealth**	3/5

Smooth, musical swagger done right. Anderson's outfit hits the sweet spot between stage-ready and storm-worthy. We think he's criminally underrated.

2

ALLEN THE ALIEN

Fun	5/5	**Originality**	5/5
Style	4/5	**Stealth**	3/5

Equal parts creepy and cool. Allen's oversized head and glowing skin are pure Fortnite madness. Weird is good, and this alien proves it.

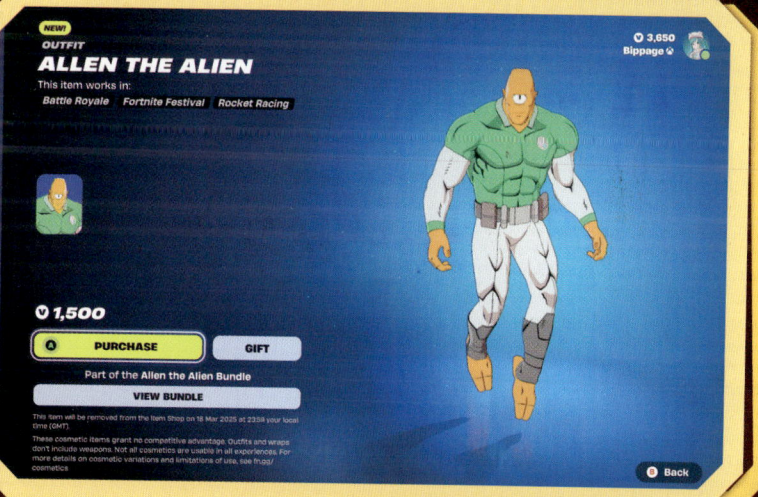

NEW!
OUTFIT
ALLEN THE ALIEN
This item works in:
Battle Royale | Fortnite Festival | Rocket Racing

1,500

PURCHASE | GIFT

Part of the Allen the Alien Bundle

VIEW BUNDLE

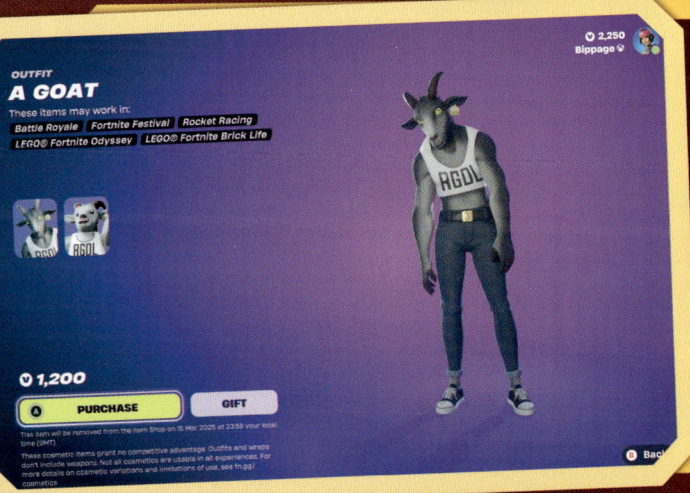

OUTFIT
A GOAT
These items may work in:
Battle Royale | Fortnite Festival | Rocket Racing
LEGO® Fortnite Odyssey | LEGO® Fortnite Brick Life

1,200

PURCHASE | GIFT

1

A GOAT

Fun	5/5	**Originality**	5/5
Style	4/5	**Stealth**	4/5

A goat by name and nature. This surreal skin is hilariously brilliant and somehow works in every setting. Weirdly majestic and the clear G.O.A.T. of this list.

TRICKY TACTICS:
HOW TO SET TRAPS IN FORTNITE

Setting traps in Fortnite isn't just about placing an item on a wall and waiting for someone to wander into it. It's about **creativity, misdirection** and a little bit of **cheeky thinking**. Whether you're playing Zero Build or classic Battle Royale, there are loads of ways to turn the battlefield into your own personal **booby-trapped** playground.

CLASSIC TRAP ITEMS [WHEN THEY'RE AVAILABLE]

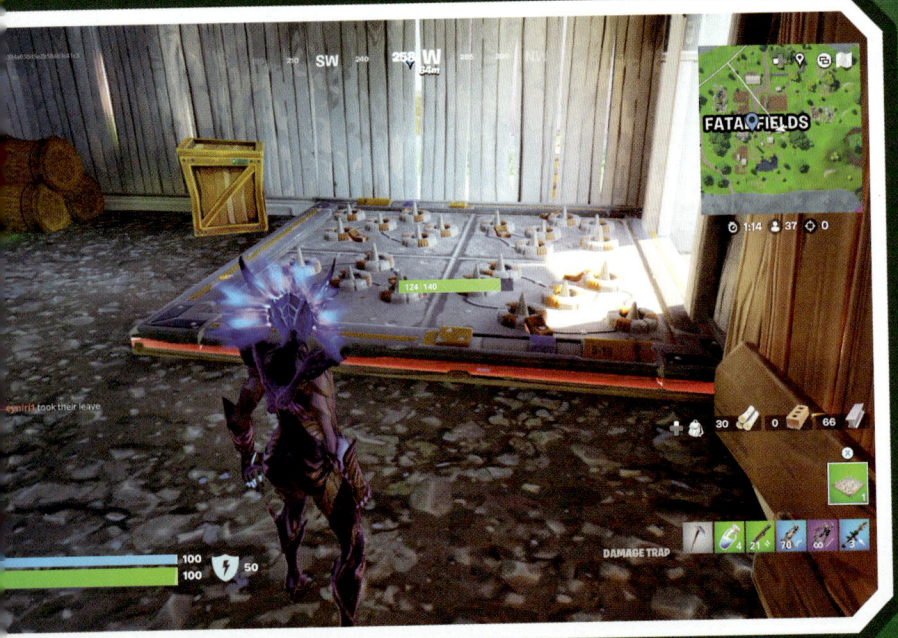

Let's start with the obvious one: actual trap items. These don't appear in every season, but when they do, they can be devastating.

Wall Traps, Floor Traps, and Ceiling Traps (also known as Spike Traps) have appeared at various points in Fortnite's history. In our view, they're one of the most satisfying ways to eliminate an opponent – especially if you manage to box them in just before triggering the trap.

We say it's always worth carrying one if they're in the loot pool. The trick is to act fast – build a small box around your opponent, place a trap, and get out before they do.

LOOT BAITING: THE CLASSIC FAKE DROP

One of the easiest and most effective homemade traps is loot baiting. Simply drop a tempting weapon, medkit or pile of ammo in an open spot and wait nearby - or stake out a llama or legendary chest. The best loot bait traps are placed in obvious locations – at the end of a corridor, in the middle of a room, or just outside a doorway.

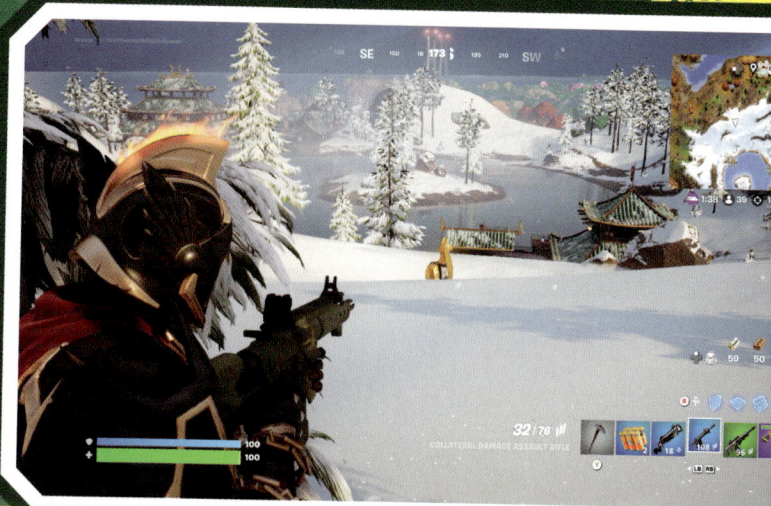

We've found that adding a Chug Jug or Legendary item to the mix increases your chances of someone falling for it. In our experience, this is a classic trick that still works surprisingly well. Just make sure you're hidden nearby and ready to strike.

DAMAGED VEHICLES: THE EXPLOSIVE DECOY

Damaged cars and bikes can become makeshift bombs. If a vehicle is on fire or close to being destroyed, a single shot can finish the job and trigger a large explosion. Park a nearly-destroyed car in a high-traffic area and wait nearby with a long-range weapon. When an opponent goes near or tries to use it – boom.

We think this tactic is especially useful in Zero Build, where players rely more on vehicles for movement. It's sneaky, satisfying, and just a little bit devious. Just be sure you're far enough away not to damage yourself.

BUSH CAMPING (YES, REALLY)

It's old-school, but it still works. Bush camping is one of the simplest traps you can set, and if you have patience, it can pay off big. Find a good bush near a loot drop or popular path, crouch inside, and wait.

In our opinion, this works best mid-game when players are rotating or distracted. Add an emote to celebrate if it works – just don't laugh too loudly.

THE FAKE REVIVE

This one works best in team modes. If you down an opponent in squads or duos, you can leave them crawling in an open space, then hide and wait for their teammates to come to the rescue. As they begin the revive, strike.

We've used this trick ourselves and we say it often works better than expected. Just make sure the bait doesn't crawl into cover before the plan works.

TRAP TUNNELS

If you're in Build Mode, try constructing a long corridor with loot placed at the far end. Most players will sprint straight towards it. Position yourself wisely and you can open fire down the tunnel, while they have nowhere to run! This plan also works if you wait near the entrance to existing tunnels that are part of the map already!

In our opinion, trap tunnels work best in late-game scenarios where opponents are rushing for heals or are low on time. The panic makes them predictable, and that gives you the upper hand.

CAMPFIRES AND EXPLOSIVES

If campfires or other healing items are in the loot pool, you can use them to lure players in. Set up a visible campfire, then place gas cans or explosives nearby. As soon as someone walks over to heal, light up the trap and enjoy the chaos. Alternatively, hide near an existing campfire in a high traffic area.

This is a more advanced move, but we think it's one of the most satisfying when it works. Bonus points if you catch more than one player in the blast.

DISGUISE BOOTHS AND NPC DISTRACTIONS

If there's a Disguise Booth nearby or a friendly NPC, you can use them as part of your trap. For example, hide near a booth and wait for an opponent to use it, then surprise them before they have a chance to react. Or start a fight near a group of NPCs and retreat behind them – the chaos often draws players in without checking corners.

We like this tactic because it turns Fortnite's own systems into part of your strategy. In our experience, it's one of the more creative ways to trap someone.

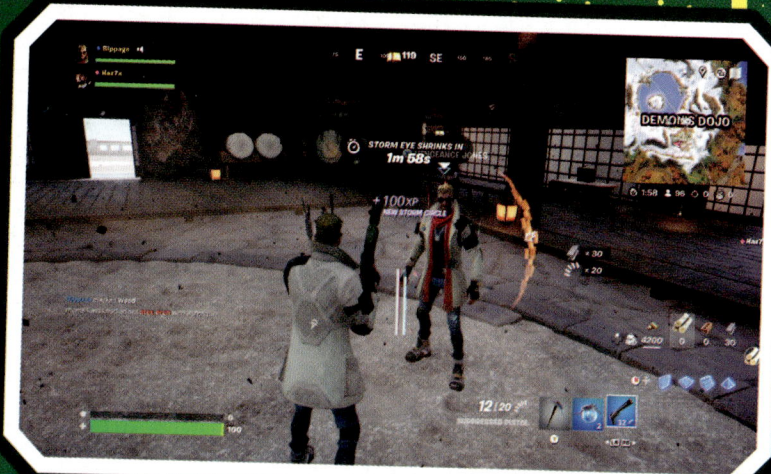

DROP TRAP TOWERS

In Build Mode, you can create a trap by luring a player up a ramp or structure, then breaking the bottom and letting them fall. This works best if the drop is high enough to cause damage or if you've placed traps or explosives at the bottom.

It's a bit of a gamble, but we say when it works, it feels like a cartoon-style victory.

HIDING INSIDE PROPS OR BUILDS

With prop disguises or well-placed builds, you can actually hide in plain sight. Box yourself into a structure that looks like a normal part of the environment. When someone enters to loot, spring out and surprise them.

In our experience, this works really well in busy POIs or when players are rushing through buildings. The key is to blend in and stay silent until the perfect moment. It's sneaky, it's silly, and it works.

VICTORY CHALLENGES

Once the Victory Royales start racking up, it's time to set some **extra challenges** for yourself. We've reviewed and rated some of the most popular challenges among Fortnite players – **how many** different ways can you win?

PACIFIST VICTORY

Secure a win without ANY eliminations. That's right, none! You will need to avoid combat, stay out of sight and try to trap your final opponent so that the storm gets them!

GAMESWARRIOR LEGEND RATING 10/10

SINGLE WEAPON WIN

You can only use one type of weapon to secure this victory. You can use different TYPES of that weapon – so, for example, different assault rifles – but the weapons class must be the same.

GAMESWARRIOR LEGEND RATING 7/10

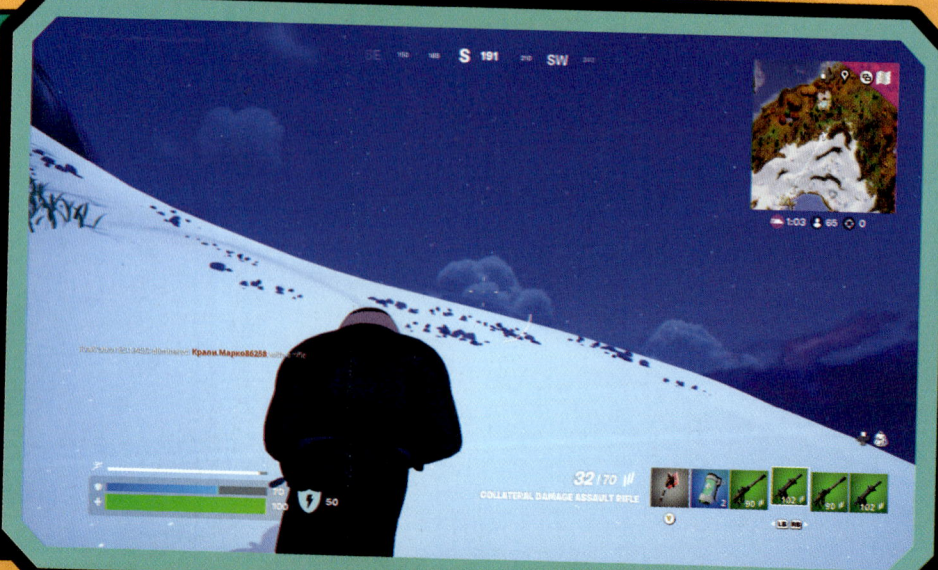

NO BUILD BATTLE

Win without building a single structure. You'll need lots of forward planning to navigate your route this way. Obviously, winning this way in Zero Build doesn't count!

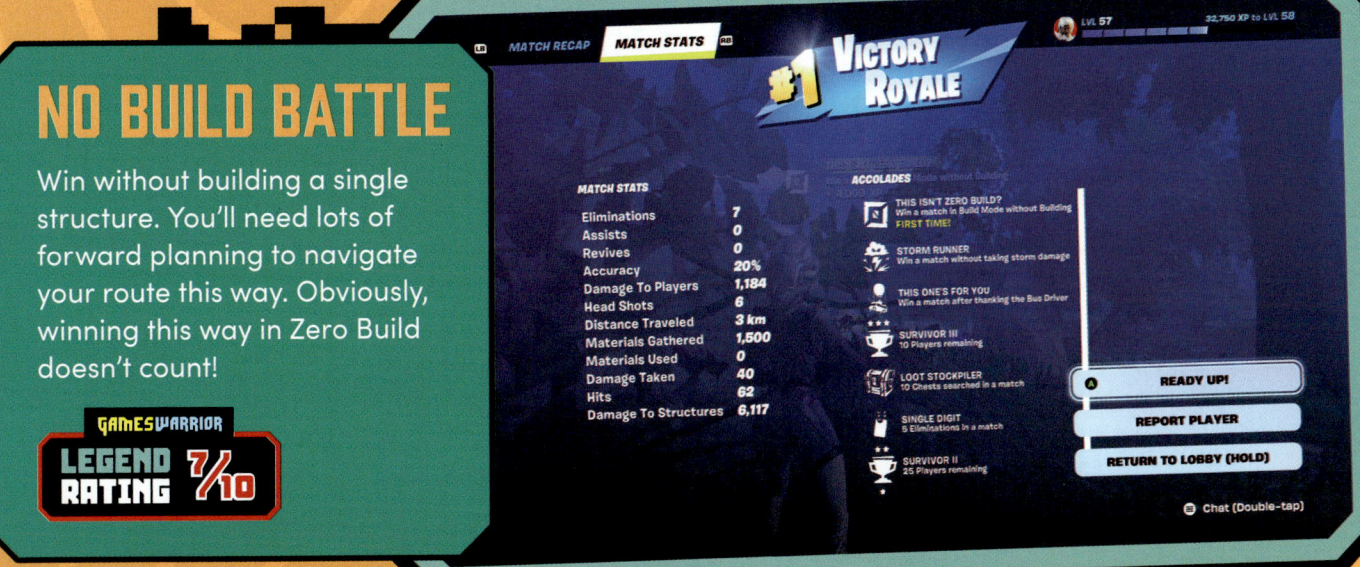

GAMESWARRIOR
LEGEND RATING 7/10

PICKAXE PROWESS

You're not allowed to pick up any weapons and must rely purely on your pickaxe to bludgeon any opponents you encounter!

GAMESWARRIOR
LEGEND RATING 10/10

NO HEALING

Avoid the use of ANY healing items to win. That means you can't even gain shield in the early stages – you must survive with only your starting 100 health and make it last right to the end!

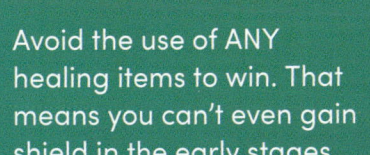

GAMESWARRIOR
LEGEND RATING 9/10

SINGLE CHEST LOOT

You're only allowed to keep the loot you find in the first chest you open. Once you have that, you can't pick up anything else. You can gather extra ammunition, but no more weapons or healing items!

GAMES WARRIOR
LEGEND RATING 9/10

NO WEAPON SWAP

You have to stick with your starting weapon until you finish the game. You don't have to pick up the first weapon you see, however, but how long will your nerve hold out before you have to pick something up and stick with it?

GAMES WARRIOR
LEGEND RATING 8/10

WALK DO NOT RUN

You know how teachers tell you off for running in the corridors? Imagine they're watching you play Fortnite! You need to win but you can ONLY walk – sprinting is not allowed, neither is getting into vehicles.

GAMES WARRIOR
LEGEND RATING 7/10

FLOOR LOOT

You can only collect loot from the floor – you aren't allowed to open ANY chests. If you find it on the floor, it's yours though.

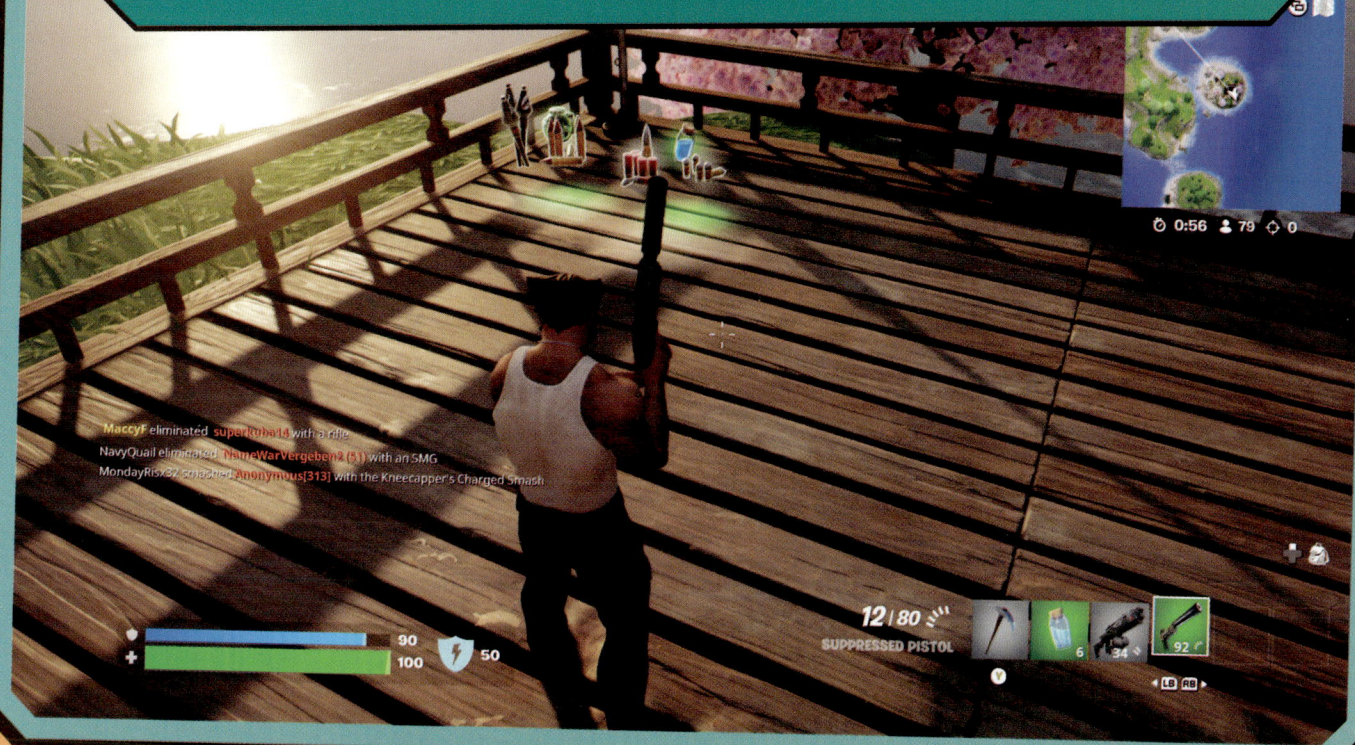

NO SHIELD HERO

Like the no healing challenge, only this time you can replenish your health all you like – but you are NOT allowed to pick up shield items!

ONE MAG WIN

You can only use one magazine per weapon. When it runs out of bullets, you can't reload and must instead dump it and find another one.

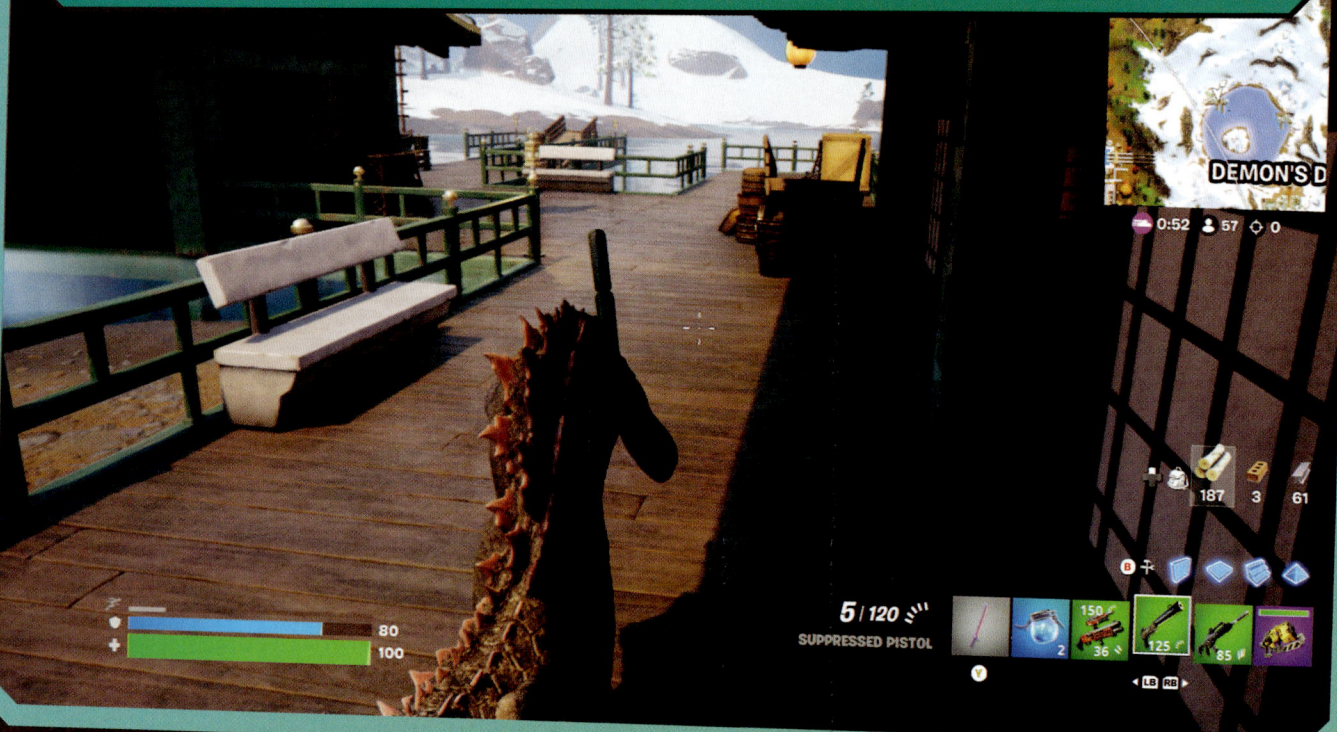

ONE SLOT SUCCESS

Ignore the full capacity of your inventory – you can only have one item in your possession at any time!

SPAWN ISLAND LOOT ONLY

Make a note of which weapons you find and pick up on Spawn Island while waiting to start. Once the game begins, you can ONLY use those weapons; you can't pick up anything you didn't have on Spawn Island!

GAMESWARRIOR
LEGEND RATING 7/10

HAN SHOT FIRST

In this mode, you can't shoot at an opponent until they have fired at you first. This stops you being able to surprise opponents, or get third party eliminations, among other things.

GAMESWARRIOR
LEGEND RATING 8/10

DRIVING DESTRUCTION

All your eliminations need to come from inside a vehicle. You can fire out of the windows if you want, or mow them down with your car, but you can't eliminate anyone while you are outside of a vehicle.

GAMESWARRIOR
LEGEND RATING 7/10

POSITIVE ENERGY

You can't use any explosive weapons or bullets in this challenge. You must win using only 'energy-based' weapons, such as lasers, shockwave grenades and so on.

GAMESWARRIOR
LEGEND RATING 9/10

DANCE MONKEY

You must do a dance emote immediately after every elimination – even if you're in the middle of a melee! This means you need to pick the timing of your eliminations carefully!

GAMESWARRIOR
LEGEND RATING 7/10

INVERTED CONTROLS

Change your controls so that they are inverted from your usual preferences and see if you can secure a win when up is down and down is up!

GAMESWARRIOR
LEGEND RATING 10/10

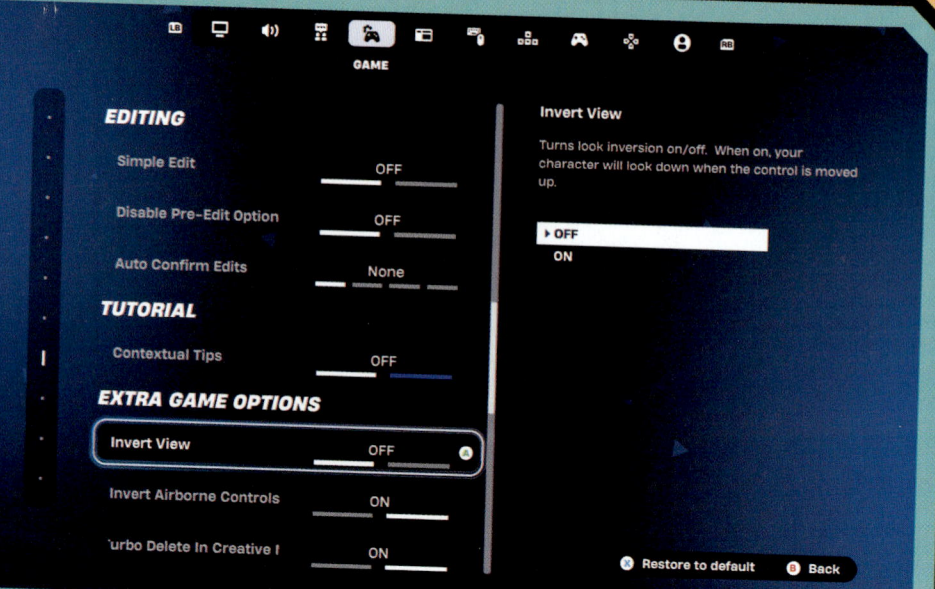

NO SCOPE

You can't use the scope on any weapon. That's not just snipers – you're not even allowed to look down the barrel of your shotguns. Can you secure a win without even aiming properly?

LAST OFF THE BUS

You must wait until you are kicked off the bus, then open your chute IMMEDIATELY. By the time you land (you can still glide to wherever you want) everyone else will have plenty of weapons and you'll be at a serious disadvantage!

DRIVE TO SURVIVE!

From transporting your squad to making a daring escape, vehicles offer creative ways to enhance your gameplay. We've ranked the most effective ways to use vehicles in Fortnite to help you decide your approach when it comes to getting behind the wheel!

TRANSPORTING YOUR SQUAD

GAMESWARRIOR USEFULNESS FACTOR 10/10

One of the most obvious benefits of vehicles is their ability to move you and your mates quickly across the map. This isn't just about speed; it's also about coordination and positioning.

BENEFITS OF SQUAD TRANSPORT

- **Quick rotations:** Vehicles let you reposition swiftly during the match, allowing you to be where the action is or to avoid dangerous zones.
- **Strategic planning:** Use vehicles to regroup in safe areas, plan ambushes, or set up coordinated attacks.
- **Resource sharing:** Moving together in a vehicle makes it easier to share loot, resources and healing items with your team.

BEST VEHICLES TO USE:

If you're in trios or squads, look for cars with enough seats for everyone. If you're playing solos or duos, sports cars are better as they only have two seats so no-one can hop in!

MAKING A QUICK GETAWAY

GAMESWARRIOR USEFULNESS FACTOR 9/10

Sometimes, the best strategy is to avoid conflict altogether. Vehicles can be lifesavers when you need to escape a hot zone or dodge an enemy ambush.

TIPS FOR A SPEEDY ESCAPE

- **Know your exit routes:** Familiarise yourself with the map so you can choose the quickest escape route when trouble arises.
- **Avoid predictable paths:** Use vehicles to take unexpected turns and throw off pursuing opponents.
- **Boost your survival rate:** A fast getaway not only saves you from a fight but also lets you regroup and plan your next move with a full squad.

BEST VEHICLES TO USE:

The bigger the better here – lorries, trucks and tanks are best. Don't worry about the lack of speed, you're looking for big vehicles that can cause damage.

REACHING HARD-TO-ACCESS AREAS

GAMESWARRIOR USEFULNESS FACTOR 7/10

Fortnite's map is filled with secret spots and high-value loot zones that can be tricky to reach on foot. Vehicles open up a whole new range of possibilities when it comes to exploring these areas.

STRATEGIES FOR EXPLORATION

- **Off-road adventures:** Some vehicles can traverse rough terrain, allowing you to access hidden or less-travelled parts of the map.
- **Sky-high drops:** Certain vehicles, like planes or gliders, can get you into elevated positions, giving you a tactical overview of enemy positions.
- **Shortcut routes:** Use vehicles to bypass long stretches of open ground, landing closer to points of interest and minimising exposure to danger.

BEST VEHICLES TO USE:

Sturdy vehicles can reach higher ground if you use the speed boost to help you, but you can't beat aircraft when it comes to getting to places other players can't!

BREAKING INTO BUILDINGS

Vehicles aren't just for transport – they can also serve as tools for gaining entry into fortified positions or buildings. This approach is especially useful when you need to surprise an enemy team or grab hard-to-reach loot.

CREATIVE ENTRY TACTICS

- **Ram and breach:** Some vehicles have enough momentum to break through barriers or walls, giving you an unexpected entry point into a building.
- **Distract and infiltrate:** While the enemy is distracted by the vehicle's impact, you and your team can slip inside unnoticed.
- **Combine with building techniques:** Use the breach as a launching pad for rapid building or cover creation once you're inside the structure.

BEST VEHICLES TO USE:

The bigger the better here – lorries, trucks and tanks are best. Don't worry about the lack of speed, you're looking for big vehicles that can cause damage.

CREATING DISTRACTIONS WITH VEHICLES

Vehicles can also be used as tools for deception. Whether you want to mislead your opponents or create chaos on the battlefield, a well-timed vehicle manoeuvre can turn the tide of battle.

DISTRACTION TECHNIQUES

- **Noise and chaos:** The sound of a revving engine or a screeching tyre can draw enemy attention away from your team's true objective.
- **Decoy movements:** Use vehicles to simulate an attack from one direction, then quickly reposition to catch opponents off guard from another angle.
- **Setting traps:** Sometimes, leading enemies into a well-planned trap with a vehicle as the bait can be the key to a successful ambush.

BEST VEHICLES TO USE:

Noisy, high-revving vehicles are best here. Sports cars rule supreme but motorbikes work well too – just don't get shot at while you're exposed!

QUIZ ANSWERS

CROSSWORD

Down 1: GLIDER
Across 3: SKIN
Down 5: JOESY
Across 8: CRANK
Across 4: MIDAS
Down 2: VAULT
Down 6: TILTED
Across 9: STORM
Down 7: TRAP
Across 10: SHOTGUN
Down 9: SLURP
Across 11: PEELY
Down 12: EMOTE

PAGE 5

WORDSEARCH

S	R	F	A	O	U	C	C	R	L	E	E	I	H
O	C	S	M	S	S	T	H	R	C	J	N	K	O
E	V	L	E	T	N	T	T	O	R	R	I	O	P
G	T	U	D	S	I	E	I	L	P	J	P	S	R
U	F	R	K	O	P	E	P	I	P	P	E	U	E
J	G	P	I	R	E	B	O	O	T	O	A	D	T
G	S	O	T	E	R	F	U	Y	P	R	R	S	I
U	N	L	O	R	E	R	U	E	T	V	G	N	N
H	O	R	O	Y	A	L	E	P	K	J	C	O	T
C	S	R	T	G	P	O	F	E	R	I	K	L	R
E	T	E	J	R	L	O	O	R	U	U	O	T	O
D	O	R	S	H	I	E	L	D	H	S	E	J	F
T	R	V	Y	E	E	Y	S	N	L	I	I	S	S
V	M	Y	Y	O	I	N	V	I	C	T	O	R	Y